ADENOIDS AND DISEASED TONSILS

LECTOR HOUSE PUBLIC DOMAIN WORKS

This book is a result of an effort made by Lector House towards making a contribution to the preservation and repair of original classic literature. The original text is in the public domain in the United States of America, and possibly other countries depending upon their specific copyright laws.

In an attempt to preserve, improve and recreate the original content, certain conventional norms with regard to typographical mistakes, hyphenations, punctuations and/or other related subject matters, have been corrected upon our consideration. However, few such imperfections might not have been rectified as they were inherited and preserved from the original content to maintain the authenticity and construct, relevant to the work. We believe that this work holds historical, cultural and/or intellectual importance in the literary works community, therefore despite the oddities, we accounted the work for print as a part of our continuing effort towards preservation of literary work and our contribution towards the development of the society as a whole, driven by our beliefs.

We are grateful to our readers for putting their faith in us and accepting our imperfections with regard to preservation of the historical content. We shall strive hard to meet up to the expectations to improve further to provide an enriching reading experience.

Though, we conduct extensive research in ascertaining the status of copyright before redeveloping a version of the content, in rare cases, a classic work might be incorrectly marked as not-in-copyright. In such cases, if you are the copyright holder, then kindly contact us or write to us, and we shall get back to you with an immediate course of action.

HAPPY READING!

ADENOIDS AND DISEASED TONSILS

MARGARET COBB ROGERS

ISBN: 978-93-5342-172-4

First Published: 1922

LECTOR HOUSE LLP
E-MAIL: lectorpublishing@gmail.com

ADENOIDS AND DISEASED TONSILS

THEIR EFFECT ON GENERAL INTELLIGENCE

BY

MARGARET COBB ROGERS, PH.D.

ARCHIVES OF PSYCHOLOGY
Edited by R. S. WOODWORTH
No. 50

Columbia University Contributions to Philosophy and Psychology

NEW YORK
April, 1922

CONTENTS

INTRODUCTION
PURPOSE

During the last decade or two there has been a growing interest among physicians in defects of the nose and throat. This interest has centered in part upon those two afflictions of childhood—adenoids and diseased tonsils,—or even tonsils that are merely enlarged. There is no doubt of the physical handicap borne by a child who is possessed of them. As a seat of inflammation, a source of infection, a hindrance to proper breathing,—in a multitude of ways they have seemed to deserve the verdict,—"Have them out." Many physicians, to be sure, have cautioned against the wholesale removal of tonsils, saying that tonsils which are large in early childhood very commonly are absorbed at an early age.

But it is not my purpose to discuss the question of the efficacy of removing adenoids and tonsils. The aim of this study is, rather, to determine experimentally whether or not there exists any causal relation between defect in this respect and lowering of intelligence level. One hears statements made both pro and con by physicians and laymen but there has been little experimental proof. It would seem to be rather useful for a physician to know in advance with how much probability of correctness he is speaking, when he advises a mother that the removal of adenoids and tonsils from the throat of her backward child will make him "bright." The question in the present case, however, is broader than that of relation between these afflictions and mental defect. We are inquiring not merely whether adenoids and tonsils are causes of sub normality or dullness, but also whether they tend to lower the intelligence quotient in general however high it may be. Would the mentally normal child with adenoids and tonsils have been superior without them, and would the superior child have been still more superior? What is the relation between adenoids and tonsils, and intelligence?

The method employed in the present experiment would seem to give it value from the point of view of the clinical psychologist. With the present emphasis upon exactitude in mental testing, investigators have become interested in problem of the constancy of the I.Q. Adenoids and abnormal tonsils have been suggested as possible factors affecting this constancy. The results of the experiment should throw some light on the question.

It should be understood that this study is concerned with general intelligence, and not with the child's efficiency as a member of society. The latter question is much broader than the one we are investigating. It includes not only intelligence, but physical state, emotional make-up, volition: in short, the personality as a whole. Success in school work for example, depends upon all of these factors. For that reason, the results to be reported here, cannot be interpreted as applying to this broader conception. We cannot say at the end whether or not the physical defects under consideration affect the child's success as a member of society. We hope to be able, however, to determine their effect upon one element of that success, namely intelligence.

In presenting the results of this experiment, the writer is especially indebted to Professor R. S. Woodworth, under whose auspices the investigation was carried out, for his interest and advice; and to Dr. Leta S. Hollingworth for the suggestion of the problem, practical aid in obtaining subjects, and constant inspiration. She is indebted to the School of Education, Teachers' College, for the provision of operative treatment for the subjects; to Mr. Mark and his officers at Public School 64; and to Superintendent O'Brien of the Manhattan Eye, Ear and Throat Hospital. It must be said that by their hearty and generous cooperation they have contributed in a large measure to whatever value this study may possess.

ADENOIDS AND DISEASED TONSILS: THEIR EFFECT UPON GENERAL IN-TELLIGENCE

CHAPTER I.

PREVIOUS LITERATURE CONCERNING THE RE-LATION OF NOSE AND THROAT DEFECTS TO IN-TELLIGENCE

There are very few experimental studies of the relation between intelligence and the two defects considered here. There are a few statistical studies, and among earlier writers especially many statements of opinion on the matter. Characteristic of the latter is the following extract from an article in the Boston Medical and Surgical Journal, March, 1886.[1]

"... it is a fact that their intelligence may become weakened and their characters changed. They do not progress in their studies at school, are generally at the bottom of the class and remain in it longer than the prescribed time.... That the impairment of intellect and want of energy manifested by these children is real, and not merely in the expression of countenance, is made evident by watching these same children after the growths have been removed. To the gratification and astonishment of the parents and teachers, the children hitherto sluggish and dull of comprehension, now make rapid progress, and their comrades soon cease to make a laughing stock of them."

The following quotation from an article by Irving Townsend, M. D., is in the same vein:[2]

"Aprosexia is the rather imposing term applied to the imperfect or arrested mental development attributed to this condition. This is denied by some authors, who claim that the dullness of comprehension and inattention are only apparent, and due only to defective hearing. A strong evidence of its reality lies in the fact that these children show most marvelous intellectual development after the removal of the growth, even in cases where deafness is not markedly improved."

[1]   F. Hooper, M. D., quoting from a paper by B. Frankel.

[2]   Adenoid Growths of the Naso-pharynx. Read before the Homeopathic Medical Society of New York, February, 1895.

A most enthusiastic denouncer of adenoids and abnormal tonsils is H. Addington Bruce. Concerning their direful effects upon the intelligence, and the magical results of their removal, he is continually reiterating:[3]

"Often a surprising development of both mental and physical power follows the removal of adenoids. In one case reported by Professor Swift, a girl of fourteen grew three inches within six months after an operation for adenoids, and at the same time showed an improvement in her school work that contrasted strikingly with the dullness that preceded it. Another, three years younger, grew six inches in about five months, and from being a sad idler was transformed into an unexpectedly attractive and bright pupil. A boy of twelve, backward both mentally and physically, likewise lost his dullness and laziness within an astonishingly short time after the impediment had been removed."

And again:

"The boy or girl suffering from adenoids[4] is usually a mouth-breather because of the difficulty experienced in breathing through the nose. But mouth-breathing means difficult breathing, and this in turn means deficient oxidation of the tissues, with a resultant lowering of vital activities generally and of the activity of the brain in particular. Accordingly, the psychologist of today insists that every adenoid-afflicted child should be given prompt medical attention, with a view to correcting the vicious mouth-breathing habit, and thus aiding the child to gain a fair start in the development of mental and physical health."

The following extracts are quoted from Burgerstein's "Handbuch der Schulhygiene":

"Bresgen und Heymann machen endlich darauf aufmerksam, dass die Ursache der Kephalalgie haufig in der Behinderung der Nasenatmung zu suchen ist, als Folgerscheinung von Verengerung der Nase bei ingen Baue des Knochengerustes, Knochenkaries und Geschwulsten, Schwelungen der Scheimhaute, akuten Schnupfen, Verstofungen der Highmorshöhle, Vergrosserung der Mandeln u. s. w."...

"Viele Kinder erscheinen schwachbegabt, ohne os zu sein, da bei denselben entweder nach behebung von Ohrenkrankheiten, nach Herstellung der freien atmung oder Gebrauch einer entsprechenden Brille die scheinbare Geistesschwache schwindet."[5]

Quotations like these, and equally unsupported by experimental evidence, might be multiplied indefinitely, especially if we look into the literature of a dozen years ago. Since they can have little authoritative value, I shall limit myself to two more specimens, one taken from the Psychological Clinic, 1916.[6]

"But when these physical defects (poor eyesight, defective hearing, adenoids, bad tonsils, etc.) are corrected so that the mind can function without any outcry

[3]　H. Addington Bruce, Psychology and Parenthood, 1916.
[4]　H. Addington Bruce in the Century Magazine, 1916—The Mind of the Child.
[5]　The italics are mine.
[6]　Psych. Clinic, 1916, 10, 45-48. Anna Johnson. The Teacher in the Retarded School.

from the physical body, these children recuperate mentally and often make greater progress than the so-called normal children in the regular grades."

The second is a quotation from Jelliffe and White, "Diseases of the Nervous System." Lee and Ferbiger, 1917, p. 903.

"An important group (of mental defects) is due to adenoid vegetations in the posterior pharynx. Under such conditions of ill health, development is impaired and does not proceed at a normal rate. With ... infected tonsils, which produce a constant toxemia, the child cannot be expected to proceed in his development with normal rapidity."

In the medical and psychological literature of the last few years, along with the growth of general discussion into the various phases of the operation itself, we find a general disinclination to take on faith the magic effect of adenectomy and tonsillectomy. This growth of critical spirit has shown itself in statistical investigations, and in studies of pedagogical and mental improvement after operation.

The statistical studies of physical defects in the schools reveal almost universally a positive relationship between school retardation and possession of adenoids and diseased tonsils. One of these was conducted by Ayres for the Backward Children Investigation of the Russell Sage Foundation in New York City.[7] The investigators examined the school records of 20,000 children from fifteen schools in Manhattan. Eight thousand of these had been examined by school physicians. The records of the physical examinations showed that 80 per cent of the children who were normal for their grade had physical defects while only about 75 per cent of the retarded children were physically defective.

This astonishing result was found upon re tabulation of the data by ages, to be due to the fact that for each defect there is a gradual falling off in frequency from the age of six up to fifteen — eye-defect, only, excepted. Since the retarded children in each grade will be the older children in that grade, and since older children have fewer defects, the retarded children will show a smaller proportion of defect.

To overcome this difficulty, Ayres used an age basis instead of a grade basis in interpreting his results. Records of all the children at the ages of 10, 12, 13, and 14 were re tabulated, a group of 3304 children, and rated as dull, normal or bright according to the grade in which they were found. The results were worked out in percentages of a group, and are shown in the following tables:

	Dull	Normal	Bright
Number of children examined	407	2588	309
Defects per child	1·65	1·30	1·07
Enlarged glands	20	13	6
Defective vision	24	25	29
Defective breathing	15	11	9
Defective teeth	42	40	34

---

[7] Psych. Clinic, 1909, 3, 71-77. The Effect of Physical Defect on School Progress.

Hypertrophied tonsils	*26*	*19*	*12*
Adenoids	*15*	*10*	*6*
Other Defects	21	11	11
Defective	75	73	68
Not defective	25	27	32

Average number of grades completed by pupils having no physical defects, compared with the number completed by those suffering from different defects:

3304 CHILDREN, 10-14 YEARS, GRADES 1-8

	Average grades completed	% lost
Children having no physical defects	4·94	
Children having enlarged glands	4·20	14·9
Children having defective vision	4·94	0
Children having defective breathing	4·58	7·2
Children having defective teeth	4·65	5·9
Children having hypertrophied tonsils	4·50	8·9
Children having adenoids	4·24	14·1
Children having other defects	4·52	8·5

Cornell reports several investigations in the Psychological Clinic, January and May, 1908. Three of these, in which children were rated on the basis of grades received in school work, are here combined to show the grades of normal children, "average" children, generally defective children, those possessing adenoids and tonsils, and the deaf.

No. of cases	Normal	Average	General Defective	Adenoids & Tonsils	Adenoids	Deaf
Allison		219				
9th St.	64	84	21		8	
Claghorn	179	252	13			
Grade in language						
9th St.	72·9	70·5	63·3		60	
Claghorn	74·4	72·7	71·4			
Grade in Arith.						
9th St.	75·5	74	70		66·7	
Claghorn	72	70	65·1			
Grade in spelling						
9th St.	75·4	72·8	64·8		65	
Grade in geography						

Claghorn	76·6	76·5	76·2		
Average of grades					
Allison	75	74	72·6	72	67
9th St.	74·6	72·4	66	63·9	
Claghorn	74·3	73·1	70·8		

An additional investigation of four classes in the same grammar grade of the Claghorn School gives the following results:

	Class 1 Bright	Class 15 Children	Class 9 Dull	Class 11 Dullest
Number of children	50	39	32	29
Normal	36	32	20	13
Defective	14	7	12	16
Percentage of normal	72	82	62·5	44·8

In the same article, Dr. Cornell gives the results of another study of Philadelphia schools, made in 1906. The study comprised a comparison of children exempt from examinations on account of high standing, with those not exempt. The results follow:

	Exempt Normal	Children Defective	Non-exempt Normal	Children Defective
9th St. Primary	56	28	39	38
Rutledge School	87	35	75	34
Allison School	128	65	81	49
Camac School	183	71	103	75
Claghorn School	193	61	127	66
	647	260	425	262
Percentage Defective	28·8		38·1	

When the four classes of bright and dull children were examined again, and the different sorts of defects compared for the groups, enlarged tonsils, adenoids, deafness, and nasal catarrh, were found to occur much more frequently among the two classes of duller children.

	Class 1 Bright	Class 15 Children	Class 9 Dull	Class 11 Dullest
Number of children	50	39	32	29

Nose and throat conditions, number defective	6	4	9	9
Tonsils	3	4	3	3
Adenoids	2	1	5	6
Deaf	2		5	1
Catarrh			2	3
Percentage of children, nose and throat defects	12	10·2	28·1	31

During the same year, another examination along the same lines was conducted in the William McKinley Primary School,[8] where a large number of dull children had been grouped in special classes.

None of these children were mentally defective, says Dr. Cornell, and only a few were really backward. The proportion of physical defect was found to be very large,—in 174 pupils, 188 physical defects (68 eye-strain, 40 nasal obstruction, 80 miscellaneous, 11 hypertrophied tonsils.) In a special class at the Wharton school, numbering 22 children, 14 of the children suffered from adenoids, associated in 3 cases with enlarged tonsils. Since no comparison is made with normal classes, this survey cannot be regarded as conclusive.

Wallin, in his book, "Mental Health of the School Child," discusses several other investigations of the relation of intelligence to physical defect. Only those studies in which were included adenoids and tonsil conditions will be reviewed here. Those by Ayres and Cornell have been described above.

In Elmira, New York, says Wallin, "an investigation of repeaters in the second grade showed that 21 per cent of those who required three years and 40 per cent of those who required four years to complete the grade had adenoids, as against only 19 per cent of those who required only two years to do the grade."

Another study described by Dr. Wallin was made by Heilman in 1907 of 1000 Camden repeaters. The correlation between pedagogical retardation and percentage of defect in each group was as follows:

Defects	Retardation				
	1 yr.	2 yr.	3 yr.	4 yr.	5 yr.
			Per Cent		
Health	16·5	21·3	28·0	19·0	37·5
Nutrition	13·4	8·9	17·2	20·2	17·5
Adenoids	6·2	7·3	8·1	9·6	7·5
Speech	5·2	5·1	4·2	10·5	20·0
Visual defects	15·5	15·9	18·2	22·8	22·8
Auditory	8·2	6·7	4·9	6·1	10·0

---

[8]   Cornell, Psychological Clinic, 2, 1909.

Burpitt[9] describes an investigation of 400 children, 200 male and 200 female, considered by their teachers to be "dull and backward, but not to fall within the meaning of feeble-mindedness as given in the Mental Deficiency Act of 1913." The children were examined for physical defects and other abnormal conditions. The author says that in 36 per cent of the cases, the cause for backwardness was found to be "inherent dullness." (The basis for judgment of inherent dullness is not given.) Adenoids and tonsillar tissue were found in 18·75 per cent of the cases, and were "more prevalent than among the children of the area as a whole."

The degree of retardation, based upon the number of school standards below normal, was ascertained for pupils who suffered from various defects. The relative retardation was expressed by the fraction $n/(A-5)$ where n = number of years retarded, and A = age. Eighteen per cent of the children were so retarded that the fraction was greater than 3-9. These were divided into two groups, — 3-9 to 4-9 and 4-9 to 5-9. The results are given in the following table:

Causes	46 children 3-9 to 4-9	24 children 4-9 to 5-9
Inherent dullness only	8	3
Inherent dullness and one or more physical defects	7	2
Irregular attendance with one or more physical defects	9	6
Irregular attendance	2	3
Adenoids only	2	0

Turning to what the author calls single causes, — present in 170 cases out of the 400, —

Causes	151 children 1-9 to 3-9	19 children 3-9 to 6-9
Irregular attendance	51	6
Adenoids	24	2
Inherent dullness	59	11

The term "cause" seems to be rather loosely used in this study. The author says concerning this,

"Dealing with physical defects first, although they amount in the aggregate to 53 per cent (omitting defective speech, which is a secondary condition), in 10 per cent only do they represent the whole cause. This is made up of those cases where the defect is of such intensity as to produce retardation in otherwise ordinary children, and of other cases of less intensity, but sufficient to weigh down the balance against those near the level of what we may call for convenience the lower limit

[9] H. R. Burpitt. Relative Degrees of Dullness and Backwardness in School Children and their Causation. Journal of Mental Science, 1916.

of normal intelligence." How he determines, without removing a defect, what the child's intelligence would be without it he does not explain.

The following table compares the physical condition of two groups, one comprised of children examined in the regular routine examinations during the year 1912,—the other a group of retarded school children, given a special examination:—[10]

	Group I		Group II	
No. of children examined	287,456		1,541	
No. with physical defects	206,720—71·9%		1,383—89·8%	
No. of defects found	226,639		2,986	
Defect	No.	%	No.	%
Anaemia			335	23·0
Malnutrition	8,303	2·9	557	36·1
Defective vision	21,078	9·3	536	34·7
Defective hearing	1,206	0·5	47	3·0
Defective nasal breathing	21,931	7·6	316	20·4
Hypertrophied tonsils	30,021	10·4	297	19·2
Defective teeth	142,168	49·4	796	51·6
Pulmonary disease	335	0·1	47	3·0
Cardiac disease	1,597	0·5	35	2·3
Average No. of defects per child	1·1		2·5	

In an investigation of 3,587 exempt and 1,418 non-exempt children in the Philadelphia schools,[11] Dr. Newmayer found the following percentages of defect:

	Exempt Children		Non-exempt Children	
Defect	No. Examined	%	No. Examined	%
Defective vision	371	10·0	171	12·0
Defective hearing	49	1·4	29	2·0
Defects of nose	54	1·5	21	1·5
Defects of throat	137	3·8	53	3·7
Orthopedic defects	25	·7	25	1·8
Mentally defective	6	·1	80	5·6
Skin diseases	918	26·0	423	30·0
Miscellaneous	214	6·0	128	9·0
Total 1,774		49·0	930	65·0

---

[10] Transactions of the International Congress on School
[11] Ayres: "Laggards in Our Schools." 1909.

It is evident from the majority of these investigations that there is some relationship between physical defects and pedagogical retardation. But whether or not the relationship is a causal one, they do not indicate. Simple co-existence of two characteristics is not necessarily significant that one is cause of the other. Plainly, though, if the removal of a physical defect is followed by improvement in the school progress, it may be argued that the presence of the defect was a causal factor in the previous retardation. The method in the few following studies, which seems to be employed to a greater degree than formerly, consists of measurement of such improvement.

The Journal of Psycho-Asthenics, March and June, 1918, contains a paper on the "Results obtained from the Removal of Tonsils and Adenoids in the Feeble-minded," by Wm. J. G. Dawson, M. D. The author starts out rather discouragingly by regarding his hypothesis as an axiom. He says,

"It is a well-known fact that hypertrophy of the tonsils and presence of adenoids may produce more or less dullness of the intellect in normal children. This is a result of the imperfect aeration of the blood which supplies the brain, on account of obstruction to respiration. In the Feeble-minded, conditions are more or less similar."

One hundred and twelve cases in the Sonoma State Home, Eldridge, California, were operated on. Of these 6 are recorded as borderline, 39 as morons, 50 as imbeciles, and 17 as idiots. Adenoids were always removed when they were present. The results of the operation are as follows:

	Number before Operation	Number after Operation	
Mouth breathing	43	31	
Eneuresis	33	32	
Sore throats	70	2	
Ear trouble	19	2	
Change in voice		38	improved
Tonsillar tissue recurred in		5	
General physical health		90	improved
		6	borderlines
		33	morons
		42	imbeciles
		9	idiots
Mental improvement from observation		27	improved
		4	borderlines
		15	morons
		7	imbeciles

1   idiot

The inaccuracy of this investigation is evident. The mental improvement was measured by "observation," which is at best inexact, and susceptible to the influence of any expectation of improvement on the part of the observer. The degree of improvement is not mentioned, nor is the time interval allowed for the appearance of such improvement. There is no control group, and consequently, no way of knowing whether the improvement was due to the removal of the defect.

A similar, though rather more careful study is reported by Dr. Charles James Bloom in the New Orleans Medical and Surgical Journal for April, 1917. Dr. Bloom's experiment consisted of eighteen months' observation on the mental and physical state following the removal of adenoids and tonsils from one hundred and fourteen children. This number was later reduced to fifty-seven, because of the fact that a number failed to return. There was no selection, all the patients being taken as admitted.

The patient's physical and mental state was recorded at the time of admission. School reports were used as an index of intelligence. From this time on the patients were examined, weighed and measured at monthly intervals.

The ages of the children ranged from four to fourteen years, inclusive. Thirty-five per cent were under six years, and sixty-five per cent, therefore, over six. Twenty-nine were boys, twenty-eight girls.

Omitting a part of the study which though interesting has no bearing upon our problem, we turn to results in the way of mental status. There were fifty-seven cases, ten of whom were under the school limit. Of the remaining forty-seven, seven sent in no report. In four, or ten percent of the forty remaining, there was no progress. In thirty-six, or ninety per cent, appreciable progress was reported. One of the four unimproved cases was syphilitic, the other, the author says was a moron.

Quotation of the teachers' reports will be of interest.

"'Some improvement.' 'Better work than previous year.' 'More effort displayed.' 'Improved wonderfully.' 'Improvement first term, not so much second.' 'Before removal, not transferred; after removal transferred.' 'Very much improved, both mentally and physically.' 'Has made progress.' 'Remarkable improvement.' 'Not transferred before removal, but after.' 'More attentive.' 'A very small but gradual improvement.' 'Am happy to tell you that he is studying more since tonsils and adenoids were removed.' 'Greatly improved.' 'Attention better.' 'More concentration.'"

In this experiment like the preceding, the judges are liable to the effect of expectation of improvement. Although the reports are more explicit, they are still couched in general terms, and not commensurable. Some reports refer to intelligence and some to pedagogical standing. There is no control group.

On the basis of these results, the author concludes:

"Children exhibiting some alternatives in the normal histology of tonsils and adenoids, give marked evidences of mental impairment." This seems to be a rather sweeping statement in consideration of the number of intellectually superior children who suffer from adenoids and diseased tonsils.

Another investigation was made by Dr. Cornell in the Philadelphia schools,[12] where seventy more or less retarded pupils in grades one to four were operated on for adenoids. According to the teachers' reports—

30 per cent improved considerably.
40 per cent improved.
25 per cent did not improve.
1·6 per cent deteriorated.
3·0 per cent deteriorated considerably.

Of those who had two chances of promotion,
6·3 per cent were promoted twice.
16·0 per cent failed twice.
33·3 per cent were promoted once.
33·3 per cent failed once.

With one opportunity,
11·0 per cent were promoted.
31·7 per cent failed.

"The promotion record was thus decidedly poor. It is possible, however, that the time for promotion came before the orthogenic effects of the operations had become effective."

The same criticisms may be brought against this investigation as were mentioned in connection with the preceding ones. Teachers' estimates of improvement, especially when such improvement is expected, and without means of measuring it objectively, are necessarily inaccurate. Again there is no control group. Of even less value are the results of an investigation in New York City by Cronin, where, out of eighty-seven cases operated on for enlarged tonsils and adenoids, "many advanced three grades during the rest of the school year, and only three lost time."

An interesting study is one that is described by John C. Simpson, M. D., in the Journal of the American Medical Association, April 1, 1916.

Dr. Simpson's results are based on a study of 571 boys of Girard College who had been operated on for adenoids and tonsils. Improvement was studied along several different lines, among them scholastic ability. For this part of the study, 45 were chosen alphabetically, 3 from each section. The only selection was for boys who were operated on long enough after coming to school to give an idea of scholastic ability; and long enough before the present study to permit a judgment as to their improvement. Monthly averages were taken of each boy up to the time of the operation and from then to the time of this study. They were based on an average of 100 per cent. As a control group, there were chosen 45 boys who had had no operation, and who lived and worked under the same conditions. They also were taken alphabetically, 3 from each section.

---

[12] Wallin: "Mental Health of the School Child." 1914.

The general average of the operative cases at the first measurement was 74·04. Of these 25, or 55·5 per cent gave an average increase in monthly standing of 4·45 after operation, while the remaining 20, or 44·5 per cent suffered a decrease of 6·09.

The average of the boys in the control group was 74·21 and for the first group after operation 74·06. "It is interesting to note," says the author, "that the standing of slightly more than half of those operated on was improved, but when compared with those not operated on, no difference is seen."

In a similar study of younger boys who had undergone the operation on entering college, and who had since had a year's study (again a group of 45), the general average was 76·61. Compared to 45 in the same classes not operated on, who had an average of 74·56, the operative group is very slightly superior, 2·05 points.

Another study of pedagogical improvement, and a valuable contribution, is that reported by A. H. MacPhail in Pedagogical Seminary for June, 1920, entitled "Adenoids and Tonsils; a Study showing how the Removal of Enlarged or Diseased Tonsils affects a Child's Work in School."

"The children studied were pupils in the Adams and Cranch Schools. Only cases were considered where there was a record of ten school months before the date of the operation, and where there was a record for at least ten month after the operation. There were thirty-one cases in all.

"School records were looked up for the ten school months preceding operation, and for each school month subsequent—up to the date of leaving school, or in the case of children still in school, up to the date of the study. There were thus longer school records for some than for others.

"The history of each case was divided into periods of ten school months each. Eighteen cases had a record of twenty months after operation and eleven cases of thirty months.

"Comparing the first period after the operation with the period before, it is found that only about one-third showed improvement, and a little over half were doing poorer work. By comparing an average of *all* work done subsequent to the operation with what was done before, it became evident that improvement in school work is not often observed until after a year from the date of the operation."

In the cases that had records for twenty months, 16 show that better work was done in the second period after the operation than in the period before.

TABLE A

TABLE SHOWING WHERE IMPROVEMENT BEGINS.

	Per Cent of cases showing improvement		
	Period 1	Period 2	Period 3
Based on 31 cases	32·2		
Based on 18 cases	33·3	66·6	
Based on 11 cases	36·3	63·5	100

Based on all groups   33·9   65·0   100

These cases were compared with a control group chosen at random. They comprised a total of 100 children who had records for four consecutive school years.

TABLE B

TABLE SHOWING HOW TIME OF IMPROVEMENT OF "OPERATED CASES" COMPARES WITH IMPROVEMENT AMONG CHILDREN AT RANDOM.

	Period 1	Period 2	Period 3
A—Per cent of 31 cases (operated upon)	32·2		
Per cent of 100 children at random	42		
B—Per cent of 18 children— 20 months (operated upon)	33·3	66·6	
Per cent of 100 children at random	42	41	
C—Per cent of 11 cases for 30 months (operated upon)	36·3	63·5	100
Per cent of 100 children at random	42	41	41

"... Immediately after operation, there seems to be a dropping off in the quality of school work done," but thereafter a marked improvement while the random group shows a comparatively static percentage of improvement from year to year. The conclusion of the author is:

"Here seems good reason to believe that the removal of diseased tonsils and adenoids is a factor in beneficially influencing the mental life of the school child. Not only is the health impaired by failure to remove these diseased parts but the mental life and activity of the child as well."

It is conceivable that pedagogical retardation might exist without any defect of intelligence. The physical effects of adenoids and tonsils might produce a tendency to fatigue, an emotional instability and consequent lack in attention, which would seriously influence the quality of school work, even though the child were of normal or superior intelligence. The relation of physical defects to intelligence has been investigated experimentally by a method which will be employed to some extent in the present investigation. In the two studies to which I refer psychological tests, rather than school standings were used as a basis for judging the intelligence. In each the effects of treatment were measured, and in one, a control group makes possible a more accurate interpretation of results.

The first of these investigations is described by Wallin.[13] It was "an attempt to determine by controlled, objective, mental measures the influence of hygiene and operative dental treatment upon the intellectual efficiency and working capacity of a squad of twenty-seven public school children in Marion School, Cleveland, Ohio (ten boys and seventeen girls), all of whom were handicapped to a consider-

[13]   Wallin: "Mental Health of the School Child." 1914.

able degree with diseased dentures or gums, and an insanitary oral cavity." The experiment extended over one year, from May, 1910, to May, 1911. The treatment included corrective work upon the teeth and mouth, and also instruction in oral hygiene, and follow-up work by an employed nurse. Five series of psychological tests were given at stated intervals during the course of the experiment. They included tests of immediate recall, spontaneous and controlled association (opposites), adding, and attention-perception (cancellation). There were six sets of each test, numbered from one to six, of equal difficulty, and given under uniform conditions. Tests 1 and 2 were given before the treatment began, and the average was taken as the "initial efficiency." The last four, or the last two, were averaged to represent the pupils' "terminal efficiency."

The results show the following influence of dental treatment upon the working efficiency of the pupils.

1. The indices of improvement are about the same for boys and girls.

2. Improvement was about the same for older and younger pupils.

3. There were great individual differences in initial proficiency and in improvement.

4. Improvement in one test does not presuppose improvement in another.

5. There is a decided gain in every test, "and not only are the gains decidedly more frequent than the losses but the largest gains are invariably emphatically larger than the largest losses."

6. The average gains in the tests were:

> Memory, 19 per cent with 8 losses and 19 gains.
> Spontaneous association, 42 per cent with 2 losses and 25 gains,
> Addition, 35 per cent with 1 loss and 26 gains.
> Controlled association, 29 per cent with 0 losses.
> Perception-attention, 69 per cent with 0 losses.
> Average gain for all tests, 57 per cent.

Unfortunately, Wallin was unable to form a control group, so that it is impossible to estimate accurately how much of this gain is due to the treatment of the defect, and how much to other causes, such as growth, etc. "But," the writer adds, "if we concede that one-half of the gain—and that is, I believe, a sufficiently liberal concession—is due to a number of extrinsic factors, such as familiarity, practice and increased maturity, the gain solely attributable to the heightened mentation resulting from the physical improvement of the pupils would still be very considerable. There is corroborative evidence to show that there was a general improvement in the mental functioning of these pupils. This evidence is supplied by the examination of the pedagogical record of scholarship, attendance and deportment. Most of the members of this experiment squad were laggards, and repeaters, pedagogically retarded in their school work from one to four years, but during the experiment year only one pupil failed of promotion, while six did thirty-eight weeks of work in twenty-four weeks, and one boy finished two years of work within the experimental year."

The second investigation was equally careful in its method. It was pursued by the Rockefeller Foundation, under the direction of E. K. Strong, with the purpose of examining the "Effects of Hookworm Disease on the Mental and Physical Development of Children."

The children were divided into five groups and tested at intervals of three and one-half months. The tests used were opposites, calculation, logical memory, memory span, hand-writing, form-board, and Binet-Simon. After the first test-series was given, the five groups were divided into sub-groups on the basis of this initial performance, so that the improvement was compared only for those sub-groups in which this was equal.

The improvement of Group A—uninfected children—proved to be greatest, and was taken as 100 per cent. On this basis, Group B—infected children not treated—showed the least improvement,—only 34 per cent. Group C—children completely cured of infection—improved 60 per cent. Group D—severely infected children, treated but not completely cured—improved 38 per cent, and Group Du—an older sub-group of D—improved 9 per cent as much as the normal children, and much less than the untreated younger children. Dr. Strong reaches the following conclusion:

"The figures show, then, that hookworm disease unmistakably affects mental development. Treatment alleviates this condition to some extent but it does not, immediately, at least, permit the child to gain as he would if he had not had the disease. And the figures apparently further show that prolonged infection may produce prolonged effects upon mentality,—effects from which the individual may never recover."

CHAPTER II.

METHOD AND PROCEDURE

The following investigation was carried on during the year and a half from October, 1919, to April, 1921. The subjects were pupils at Public School 64, Manhattan, or patients at the Manhattan Eye, Ear and Throat Hospital. All were boys, between the ages of six and fourteen years. The testing in the study of improvement was done by the investigator, assisted by three other examiners, all competent and experienced in the technique of giving psychological tests.

A STATISTICAL STUDY

In addition to the more lengthy experiment, a statistical study was made, comparing the intelligence levels of two groups of children, the one selected for the presence of tonsils, the other for freedom from them. These two groups were obtained from a large group of 530 children whose I.Q.'s were gained from the records of Public School 64, where, so far as possible, all children are tested upon entering school. We had, therefore, a group unselected for intelligence level.

All the children for whom we had I.Q.'s were examined by the school nurse or physician. On the basis of this examination the two groups were selected. The tonsil group consisted of those cases which in the opinion of the nurse or doctor, were pronounced enough to deserve treatment. The normal group was composed of those who were not defective, or in whom the defect was so slight as not to demand treatment. The two groups were arranged each in a surface of distribution according to the I.Q.'s of the members. The results of the distribution appear in Table I, and in Figs. I. and II.

A STUDY OF IMPROVEMENT AFTER TREATMENT

The method employed here is based on the hypothesis that if a physical defect is the cause of retardation in mental or physical development, removal of the cause will tend to lessen the retardation. In other words, if a child's working efficiency is lowered by the effects of adenoids and bad tonsils, their removal should, unless such lowering be permanent, be followed after a reasonable time by an improvement. But improvement in efficiency, following the removal of adenoids and tonsils proves nothing unless we shall compare it with the change in efficiency of a control group, whose members have not been operated on, and who thus still suffer from the effects of the growths.

SELECTION OF CASES

The selection of the children for the experiment was effected in the following manner. The teachers at Public School 64 were asked to report any cases which had come to their notice, as being seriously afflicted with adenoids and diseased tonsils. In this way a fairly large group was obtained. The parents of the children were visited with the purpose of obtaining permission for examination and operation at the Post Graduate Hospital. It was fairly easy to obtain permission to have the children examined. They were taken in groups of four or five to the clinic, the experimenter attending in person every examination in order to learn from the doctors the degree of the defect. As a result of this method, we discarded all those cases where there was any doubt as to the serious nature of the defect.

From the large group examined, we were finally successful in securing operative treatment for 10 children. Discarding the cases where defect was slight, there remained a number of children who, for one reason or another, did not undergo operation. In some instances the parents refused their permission, in some they failed to keep appointments, in one or two there was sickness in the family, and in a number the hospital was overcrowded and could not receive the children. All members of this group were examined, — to the number of fifty-six, and from them the control group was finally selected.

Since we were unable to secure a large test group from Public School 64, the experiment was continued at the Manhattan Eye, Ear and Throat Hospital where opportunity was given for testing the children after they had been admitted for operation. In order to be sure that in each case the defect was sufficiently pronounced to render decisive the results of the experiment, each child's card was examined. Only those children were included who were undergoing operation for both adenoids and tonsils.

It may be here remarked that mental tests were given to these children on the morning of operation, and in some cases only a short time before it. The possibility suggests itself, therefore, that the results of the tests may have been influenced by excitement or fright on the part of the patients. Actually, however, this did not seem to be the case. The children were perfectly cheerful and showed no signs of nervousness. The tests were given in a waiting room with the door closed so that any disturbing sights and sounds were eliminated. The possible lowering of the performance by the causes mentioned would tend to exaggerate the improvement shown by the retests, so that in the light of the results, it will be seen that they could have had little effect.

The test group, then, was composed of forty members; ten from Public school 64, who received operation at the Post Graduate Hospital, and the remaining thirty from various schools throughout the city, patients at the Manhattan Eye, Ear and Throat Hospital. The control group of forty was selected as previously described, and the pairs were arranged so as to have the ages of the members of one pair as nearly as possible the same.

THE TESTS

Since the main interest of this investigation lies with intellectual development, two tests of intelligence were given: namely, Terman's revision of the Binet test, and Healy's Picture Completion Test, number II. The starred Terman was always used, since it was necessary to economize time.

It was expected that improvement in general health would probably follow the removal of the defects. This physical gain should come to light in increased height and weight. In every case, therefore, height and weight were measured.

It is conceivable that adenoids and tonsils might have no effect upon general intelligence, and yet might cause a noticeable pedagogical retardation, simply as a result of the child's physical handicap, tendency to fatigue and consequent defect in attention or sustained effort. In order to gain some measure of this physical factor, strength of grip and speed in tapping were found. An effort was made, also, to obtain teachers' estimates of the pedagogical rankings, but this was for the most part unsuccessful, since in many cases teachers misunderstood directions, and in others the tests were made too soon after the opening of school for any such estimates to be possible.

The tests described above were given before the operation to each child in the test group, allowing as short an interval as possible between test and operation. In the case of the Manhattan Hospital children, test and operation fell on the same day. In no case did the interval exceed ten days. The members of the control group were tested, each one within a week of his partner.[14]

Six months after his first test, each child was retested, whenever possible. Since some children had dropped out of the groups for one reason or another, the final number in each group was twenty-eight. It was necessary to rearrange the control cases somewhat in order to fill in spaces left vacant by those who were lost. In this rearrangement, the effort was made, 1. to pair cases whose ages were approximately the same; 2. to pair cases whose first tests were dated fairly close together. Since all the children were tested and retested under approximately the same conditions, this rearrangement will probably not greatly influence the results. The tests were always given in the same order.

The following table shows a list of the two groups, as originally paired, and as finally rearranged, with dates of tests and retests. Dates of operation are given for the first group.

	Test Case				Original Control			Final Control	
	Test I	Op.	Test II		Test I	Test II		Test I	Test II
JB	10-15-19	10-20-19	lost	SS	10-15-19	4-15-20			
LL	10-15-19	10-20-19	4-15-20	LJ	10-15-19	lost	SS	10-15-19	4-15-20
HK	10-30-19	11-6-19	4-30-20				MG	10-21-19	4-30-20

[14]   In a few cases where the operation was postponed after just previous to the operation. Since both cases were retested, practice effect is of no great importance.

MS	11-11-19	11-12-19	5-17-20			AA	11-20-19	5-17-20
GF	12-11-19	12-26-19	6-11-20			SD	12-4-19	6-11-20
RJ	12-16-19	12-30-19	6-16-20			NF	12-10-19	5-14-20
JJ	12-16-19	12-30-19	6-16-20			ML	12-5-19	6- 9-20
AG	1-15-20	1-16-20	7-15-20			LP	1-15-20	7-15-20
IK	2-14-20	2-16-20	8-11-20			AL	2-14-20	8- 2-20
HG	2-10-20	2-11-20	moved	control removed				
AC	2-11-20	2-12-20	8- 2-20			JF	2-11-20	8- 3-20
CL	2-26-20	3-1-20	8- 3-20			JF	2-26-20	8- 3-20
MR	2-26-20	3-1-20	moved	control removed				
SR	2-26-20	2-27-20	8- 3-20			PG	2-26-20	8- 3-20
IK	3-17-20	3-17-20	moved	control removed				
AO	3- 8-20	3-8-20	9-20-20			SK	3- 9-20	9-24-20
RB	3- 8-20	3-8-20	moved	control removed				
DT	3- 8-20	3-8-20	mastoid	control removed				
AL	3- 9-20	3-9-20	moved	control removed				
JD	3- 9-20	3-9-20	9-23-20			DD	3-11-20	9-16-20
LS	3- 9-20	3-9-20	9-25-20			KS	3-16-20	9-24-20
JB	3-12-20	3-12-20	moved	control removed				
HS	3-13-20	3-13-20	9-21-20			MR	3-15-20	9-15-20

AM	3-13-20	3-13-20	9-20-20	JM	3-13-20	lost	HH	4- 6-20	10-1-20
SO	3-18-20	3-18-20	9-22-20	SS	3-22-20	wrong boy	MA	3-23-20	9-23-20
IF	3-18-20	3-18-20	9-23-20			(adenoids	PK	3-22-20	9-21-20
AD	3-19-20	3-19-20	9-20-20	LC	3-22-20	(removed	IB	3-23-20	9-24-20
JR	3-19-20	3-19-20	moved	IB	3-23-20	9-24-20			
JN	3-20-20	3-20-20	moved	MA	3-13-20	9-23-20	LF	3-20-20	10-1-20
HS	3-20-20	3-20-20	9-21-20				SB	3-25-20	9-21-20
II	3-26-20	3-26-20	9-24-20				BF	4- 5-20	10-1-20
UF	3-27-20	3-27-20	9-29-20				LF	4- 7-20	10-1-20
SM	3-27-20	3-27-20	9-30-20				LG	4- 6-20	10-1-20
AM	3-29-20	3-29-20	9-29-20				BG	4- 6-20	10-1-20
CK	3-29-20	3-29-20	9-29-20				NF	4- 7-20	10-1-20
FB	3-30-20	3-30-20	9-29-20				JF	3-26-20	10-1-20
AA	3-30-20	3-30-20	9-23-20						
LS	3-31-20	3-31-20	moved		control	removed	MA	4- 5-20	9-30-20
FT	3-31-20	3-31-20	9-28-20						
LP	4- 1-20	4-1-20	moved	HH	4- 6-20	10- 1-20			

CHAPTER III.

DISCUSSION OF THE RESULTS

STATISTICAL STUDY

The statistical study compared two groups of cases in respect to I.Q. These groups were selected from one large group, on the basis of presence or absence of tonsillar defect. The tonsil group was composed of 236 cases, and the normal group, of 294. The distribution of the two groups according to intelligence is set forth in Table I, and in Figs. I and II.

TABLE I

I.Q.	Tonsil Group No. of Cases	Tonsil Group Per cent of Cases	Normal Group No. of Cases	Normal Group Per cent of Cases
40- 50	2	·8	0	0
50- 60	1	·4	2	·7
60- 70	7	2·9	4	1·4
70- 80	21	8·9	29	9·8
80- 90	45	19·0	52	17·7
90-100	80	33·9	107	36·4
100-110	55	23·3	67	22·8
110-120	17	7·2	24	8·1
120-130	6	2·5	9	3·0
130-140	2	·8	0	0
140-150	1	·4	0	0
Average	94·9		95·4	
Median	95·3		95·6	
Q	8·705		8·27	
σ	14·4		12·2	

From these it is evident that the two groups are practically equal in intelligence. The average I.Q. for the normal group is 95·4, as compared with 94·9 for the tonsil group. The medians are equally close,—95·6 in the normal group and 95·3 with the tonsil cases. The difference in variability is negligible, Q being 8·705 and σ 14·4 in the tonsil group, while in the normal Q is 8·27 and σ 12·2. The two cases with the lowest I.Q.'s were tonsil cases, but the three highest I.Q.'s also belong in this group.

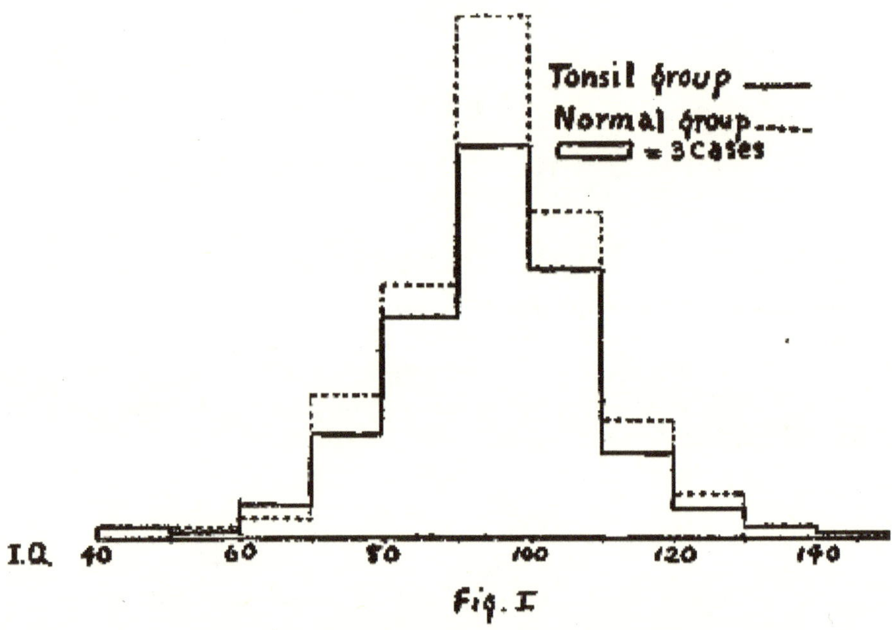

Fig. 1. Distribution of I.Q.'s. Number of cases.

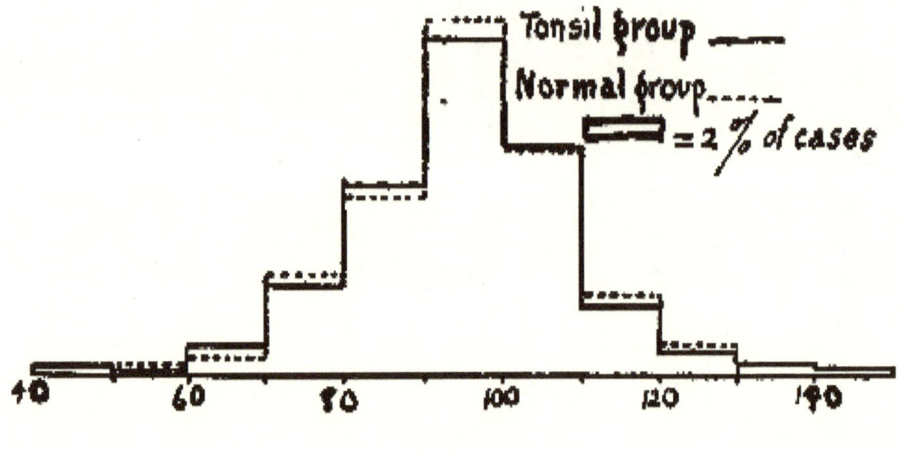

Fig. 2. Distribution of I.Q.'s by percentage of total number of cases in the group.

If the frequencies are expressed in terms of per cent of the total number of cases in the group, the two may be compared further. The following details are noticeable.

I.Q.	Per cent of Tonsil Group	Per Cent of Normal Group
Below 70	4·1	2·1
Below 90	32·0	29·6
Above 110	10·9	11·1
Above 120	3·7	3·0
Above 130	1·2	0

In other words, in the percentage of cases below normal intelligence, the tonsil group exceeds by 2·4 per cent. The percentage of defective cases is also slightly greater in the tonsil group—the difference here being 2 per cent. The normal group has a negligible predominance of bright cases,—only two-tenths of one per cent difference, while with the very superior cases, the tonsil group again exceeds,—by 1·2 per cent. The per cent of the tonsil group which reaches or exceeds the median of the normal is 49 per cent.

These figures seem to indicate remarkable similarity between the two groups considered. The two distributions are almost identical. While the slight predominance of cases below normal mentality in the tonsil group may indicate a very feeble tendency toward coincidence of tonsillar defect and mental dullness, it does not seem large enough to be at all significant. This is especially true when we consider that the tonsil group exceeds in superior children. If we allow the preceding contention of coincidence between dullness and tonsils, must we not argue here in the same manner for a tendency toward coincidence of superiority and tonsils?

The chief source of error in this part of the study is the fact that the throat examinations were not conducted by the same person throughout the investigation. For this reason there must have been some slight disagreement as to what should constitute a reportable case. In the event, then, of a positive relationship between tonsil defect and lowering of the intelligence quotient, placement of normal tonsils in the "tonsil" group, and of diseased tonsils in the "normal" group would raise the first, and lower the second, thus tending to conceal the difference between the two. On the other hand, the cases where disagreement would occur would naturally be those of slighter defect, in which the intellectual retardation would be less likely to occur, so that the result would probably be merely an increased height at the overlapping portion of the curves, with no change at the ends.

In any case, the two examiners had worked together previously, so that each must have been somewhat familiar with the opinions of the other. They were aware, also, that pronounced tonsillar defect was what we were attempting to detect. However this may be, there must always be some disagreement in diagnosis. When this is allowed for, the results of the investigation may be taken for what they are worth. Contrary to expectation, there seems to be very little difference in intelligence between a group of children whose throats are normal, and one in whom the tonsils are diseased or badly enlarged.

STUDY OF IMPROVEMENT AFTER OPERATION

The complete results of the tests and retests are collected in Table II, where each control case is listed immediately below its respective test case, and where age, height, weight, grip, tapping rate, I.Q., and score in Healy Picture Completion are shown. From these data the more detailed observations have been made. The improvement of each child in the various tests has been computed, and a comparison drawn between the two groups. As we have previously stated, any improvement shown by the test group in excess of that of the control group, may be looked upon as significant.

Let us consider first the improvement of the children in general health, as shown by height and weight. In Tables III and IV we have tabulated the results, in such shape as to permit of comparison. An inspection of these tables will establish the fact that after a six months' interval, the test group shows, in respect to height and weight, a very slight gain over the control group. In weight, the average of the amounts by which the test group gains exceed the control group gains is 1·37 lbs., and in height, only ·16 inches. The medians of these amounts are 1·2 lbs. and ·2 inches respectively. Comparing the improvements for the two groups, we find that in the case of the weights, the smallest gain (a loss of 1·2 lbs.) occurs in the control group, while the largest gain (10·7 lbs.) is in the test group.

TABLE II. RESULTS OF TESTS

Blank spaces indicate where tests were omitted for one reason or another

N	Age		Weight lbs.		Height in.		Grip, Kg. best hand	
	1	2	1	2	1	2	1	2
1	7- 7	8- 1	50·4	54·2	46	47·6	13	12
1C	8- 1	8- 7	53·5	57·2	46·4	47·8	11	13
2	6- 9	7- 3	40·9	42·9	42·6	41·1	9	9
2C	7- 1	7- 7	52·3	57·4	45·2	47	10	12
3	8-	8- 6	55	59·5	47	48·4	12·8	14·5
3C	9- 9	10- 3	61·5	62·9	51·7	52·9	14	15
4	8-10	9- 4	51·1	54·2	47·5	49·2	9	
4C	9-10	10- 4	49·4	51	48·9	52	9·5	
5	6- 1	6- 7	45	47	44·9	45·2	11	
5C	8- 2	8- 8	56·2	57	46·6	48·1	12	

6	5- 2	5- 8	43·8	44·5	43·1	43·9	8	
6C	7- 1	7- 7	50·6	52·5	45·4	47·3	10·5	
7	6- 7	7- 1	39·9	41	42·9	44·8	7	6·5
7C	6- 7	7- 1	38·4	38·7	41·9	43·2	9	10
8	8- 6	9-	60·8	63·3	50·8	51·8	10	
8C	8- 5	8-11	45·4	52·1	46·8	47·6	15	16
9	9- 4	9-10	50·6	53·2	48·1	49·4	10·5	13
9C	9- 6	10-	59·8	61·4	51·9	55·2	16·5	21
10	6- 7	7- 1	48·9	51·4	46·1	47·7	12·5	11
10C	7-	7- 6	47·1	47·5	45·6	47·2	10	15
11	6- 7	7-	47·8	47·5	45·8	47·7	11	15
11C	6- 8	7- 1	41·6	42·5	43·6	44·9	11·5	11·5
12	7- 8	8- 2	48	52·5	44·8		14	
12C	7- 1	-8	41	44·5	41·5	43·3	6	4·5
13	13- 3	13-10	90	98	61·5	65	26·5	28·5
13C	14- 6	15-	74·7	76·8	56·8	57·8	22	23
14	11- 9	12- 4	56	62	51	51·6	16	15
14C	11-10	12- 4	81·9	86	57·9	58·3	22	24
15	10- 3	10-10	57·5		51·1			15·5
15C	10- 1	10- 7	67·2	70·3	50·1	51	15	15·5
16	10- 9	11- 3	56	57	51·6	52·3	19	17·5
16C	10- 9	11- 3	51·2	50	48·7	49·5	10	10
17	8- 1	8- 7	57		48·7		14	
17C	7-10	8- 4	45·3		44·8		10	8·5
18	7- 2	7- 8	58·2		47·3		11	
18C	6-11	7- 5	45·3	47	46·7	47·1	8	6·5

N								
19	11- 4	11-10	90	96·3	57·7	59	22	21
19C	7-11	8-5	52·4	54·4	46·7	47·2	15	12
20	7- 1	7- 7	44·2		47·2		11	
20C	7- 3	7-10	61·3	66	49·6	55	15	12·5
21	11-	11- 6	70·7	76·5	54·1		16·5	16·5
21C	10- 1	10- 7	62·4	67	49·6	50·4	19	15
22	10- 9	11- 3	73·3		53	56·4	18	22·5
22C	11- 7	12- 1	70·7	80·5	56·8	58·1	19·5	21·5
23	8- 7	9- 1	51·7		47·8		11·5	15·5
23C	8-11	9- 4	64·1	66·5	51·4	53·1	14·5	14
24	9- 8	10- 2	58·5	62·5	51		19	20
24C	10- 2	10- 8	60	61	50·1	51·5	15	15
25	10- 1	10- 7	55·5	59·5	50	50·8	14	
25C	10-10	11- 4	63·3	63·8	50·2	50·9	12·5	21·5
26	9- 8	10- 2	63·8	74·5	51·6	54·3	14	
26C	10- 4	10- 9	64·2	67	51·4	52·3	20	16·5
27	6- 7	7- 1	43·7		45·4		9	6
27C	6- 3	6- 9	41	44	44·6	45·4	8	9
28	12-11	13- 5	71·3	75·5	54·9	55·8	23·5	21
28C	13- 8	14- 2	74·2	79·8	53·4	54·5	21	

TABLE II. RESULTS (CONTINUED)

Blank spaces indicate where tests were omitted for one reason or another

N	Tapping, 1/2 min. best hand		I.Q.		Healy, Score	
	1	2	1	2	1	2
1	135	120	82	83	-25	-2
1C	106	115	80	76	-50	-16

2	105	112	107	114	28·5	30
2C	152	114	91	96	3	-11
3	136	139	94	91	21·5	22·5
3C	135	129	82	85	17	19
4	103		96	96	8·5	
4C	109		83	85	33	
5	110		95	99	-25	
5C	156		114	117	40·5	
6	110		95	101	-33	
6C	126		88	89	-32	
7	125	113	91	99	6	-28
7C	105		95	99	4·5	27·5
8	113	110	91	86	32·5	
8C	131	101	98	104	4	23
9	149	135	83	93	3·5	10·5
9C	144	150	87	90	34	55
10	68+ 74	88+ 82	110	109	-12	6·5
10C	70+ 54	135+109	104	100	27	65
11	125+ 90	98+ 87	103	100	- 8	6
11C	155+125	101+107	101	102	-29	-3·5
12	98+69		98	95	20	21
12C	102	84	98	101	-10	-12
13	160+165	142+134	70	78	43	42
13C	150+109	122+ 94	66	64	- 1·5	30·5
14	190+172	138+130	96	107	12·5	48·5

14C	175+152	175+164	140	137	- 5	25·5
15	172+167	170+156	97	94	7	25
15C	140+115	137+115	78	79	1	42·5
16	145+131		65	73	49	47·5
16C	145+99	135+135	74	82	30	37
17	90+89	150+100	71	77	29·5	12
17C	125+116	121+ 97	96	99	1·5	15
18	133+115	135+111	98	98	-13·5	-12
18C	100+ 99	84+ 74	90	94	-32	-28
19	168+136		96	101	57·5	49
19C	100+115	118+ 92	98	98	-22	-11
20	105+115	110+ 93	106	102	0	-11
20C	150+120	155+149	118	131	30	35
21	152+111	132+125	64	67	20	32
21C	140+136	138+110	86	97	70·5	58·5
22	164+148	183+141	91	100	48·5	43·5
22C	120+116	157+127	63	62	34·5	33·5
23	150+119	141+136	85	94	49·5	68
23C	122+115	140+110	81	96	4	25
24	157+136	142+126	131	124	54·5	63
24C	155+135	155+100	89	92	31·5	59·5
25	140+127	150+119	77	76	8	25
25C	148+134	151+135	145	137	29·5	29
26	137+113	138+117	80	76	22·5	7
26C	125+105	125+ 79	90	88	56	61·5

27	108+ 92	97+ 92	110	109	-25	15
27C	115+105	112+109	72	96	2	27·5
28	150+148	162+143	81	84	29·5	73·5
28C	178+148	170+163	95	98	64·5	51·5

We have therefore:

28 pairs of I.Q's to be compared
21 pairs of weights
19 pairs of heights
16 pairs of grip measurements
20 pairs of tapping speeds
24 pairs of Healy Completion scores.

Again, in only five pairs does the gain of the control exceed that of the test case, while in the remaining sixteen pairs the gains of the test cases are greater than those of their respective controls. The greatest loss of test as compared to control is 4·2 lbs., while the largest gain is 7·9. It would seem then, that after a six months' interval a child who has been operated on for adenoids and tonsils will tend to show a slightly greater increase in weight than a child who continues to suffer from the defects. The very small group renders this conclusion far from assured. Since it doubtless takes some little time to recover from the effects of the operation, and since there is comparatively little gain in weight in a six months' interval, it would be well to extend the experiment over another year. For the greater reliability of results, some degree of after-care should be given the operative cases, the control cases of course receiving the same treatment. While this was impracticable in the present study, it happened that three pairs of cases were members of a nutrition class, and therefore underwent some hygienic treatment. In one pair, (no. 11) the test case lost ·3 of a pound, while the control gained ·9. The test cases of pairs 7 and 10 gained ·8 lb. and 2·1 lbs. respectively, over and above their controls. However, these three cases alone are of little significance.

A study of increase in height suffers even more than one of weight gains from the short interval which elapsed between measurements. Normally, there is very little growth in six months. There are only nineteen pairs of cases in this portion of the study, a fact which renders it of even less value. However, results are offered for what they are worth. The smallest increase in height (·3 in.) is in the test group, while the greatest growth (3·5 in.) is also in the test group. There is, however, a gain of 3·3 inches in the control group as well as one of only ·4 inches. There are seven pairs in which the test group growth is less than that of the controls, one in which the two are equal, and in the remaining eleven the growth of the test cases exceeds that of the controls. The variability

TABLE III

GAIN IN WEIGHT, 6 MONTHS, 21 PAIRS

N[*]	Test Group (A)			Control Group (B)			Lbs.
	Test 1	Test 2	Gain	Test 1	Test 2	Gain	A-B
8	60·8	63·3	2·5	45·4	52·1	6·7	-4·2
2	40·9	42·9	2·0	52·3	57·4	5·1	-3·1
28	71·3	75·5	4·2	74·2	79·8	5·6	-1·4
6	43·8	44·5	·7	50·6	52·5	1·9	-1·2
11	47·8	47·5	-·3	41·6	42·5	·9	-1·2
1	50·4	54·2	3·8	53·5	57·2	3·7	·1
7	39·9	41·0	1·1	38·4	38·7	·3	·8
9	50·6	53·2	2·6	59·8	61·4	1·6	1·0
12	48·0	52·5	4·5	41·0	44·5	3·5	1·0
14	56·0	62·0	6·0	81·9	86·0	4·9	1·1
5	45·0	47·0	2·0	56·2	57·0	·8	1·2
21	70·7	76·5	5·8	62·4	67·0	4·6	1·2
4	51·1	54·2	3·1	49·4	51·0	1·6	1·5
10	48·9	51·4	2·5	47·1	47·5	·4	2·1
16	56·0	57·0	1·0	51·2	50·0	-1·2	2·2
24	58·5	62·5	4·0	60·0	61·0	1·0	3·0
3	55·0	59·5	4·5	61·5	62·9	1·4	3·1
25	55·5	59·5	4·0	63·3	63·8	·5	3·5
19	90·0	96·3	6·3	52·4	54·4	2·0	4·3
13	90·0	98·0	8·0	74·7	76·8	2·1	5·9
26	63·8	74·5	10·7	64·2	67·0	2·8	7·9
Av·	56·86	60·61	3·76	56·24	58·60	2·39	1·37
M			3·80			1·9	1·2
75%ile			5·80			4·6	3·1
25%ile			2·00			·9	0·1
Q			1·90			1·85	1·5
P. E. (distribution)			1·76			1·39	1·63
P. E. (average)			±·38			±·30	±·48
							Av. =2·85 P. E.
							M. =2·80 P. E.

of the test group growth is greater than that of the control group. The three nutrition pairs show the following records of growth,—in number 7, the test case shows a growth of ·6 in. more than his control. Number 10 is the pair in which the growth is equal. In number 11 the test case again exceeds in growth by ·6 of an inch.

More reliable than height and weight considered separately, as an index of physical welfare, is weight in relation to height and age. Table V shows the improvement in this relationship for the two groups. The numbers in columns 1, 2, 4 and 5 show the per cent under or over weight of the individual cases, in relation to their respective heights and ages. The authority upon which the figures are based, is the table published by the American Child Health Association, giving standard weights for height and age in boys.

There was an average loss of ·28 per cent in the weight-height-age relationship for the test group, and of 2·11 per cent for the control group. The average improvement of the test group in excess of the control group is, then, 1·83 per cent. The median improvement of test group over and above control is 4·00 per cent. The test group is more variable than the control in improvement. The greatest improvement, 8 per cent, is found in both groups.

TABLE IV

GAIN IN HEIGHT—6 MONTHS, 19 PAIRS

N[†]	Test Group (A)			Control Group (B)			Inches
	Test 1	Test 2	Gain	Test 1	Test 2	Gain	A–B
9	48·1	49·4	1·3	51·9	55·2	3·3	-2·0
4	47·5	49·2	1·7	48·9	52·0	3·1	-1·4
5	44·9	45·2	·3	46·6	48·1	1·5	-1·2
6	43·1	43·9	·8	45·4	47·3	1·9	-1·1
2	42·5	44·1	1·6	45·2	47·0	1·8	-·2
28	54·9	55·8	·9	53·4	54·5	1·1	-·2
16	51·6	52·3	·7	48·7	49·5	·8	-·1
10	46·1	47·7	1·6	45·6	47·2	1·6	0
25	50·0	50·8	·8	50·2	50·9	·7	·1
1	46·0	47·6	1·6	46·4	47·8	1·4	·2
3	47·0	48·4	1·4	51·7	52·9	1·2	·2
8	50·8	51·8	1·0	46·8	47·6	·8	·2
14	51·0	51·6	·6	57·9	58·3	·4	·2
7	42·9	44·8	1·9	41·9	43·2	1·3	·6
11	45·8	47·7	1·9	43·6	44·9	1·3	·6
19	57·7	59·0	1·3	46·7	47·2	·5	·8
26	51·6	54·3	2·7	51·4	52·3	·9	1·8
22	53·0	56·4	3·4	56·8	58·1	1·3	2·1
13	61·5	65·0	3·5	56·8	57·8	1·0	2·5
Av.	49·26	50·79	1·53		50·62	1·36	·16
M			1·4			1·3	·2
75%ile			1·9			1·75	·65
25%ile			·78			·8	-·43

Q	·56		·48	·54
P. E. (distribution)	·53		·44	·44
P. E. (average)	±·12		±·10	±·16

Av.=1 P. E.
M=1·25 P. E.

The greatest loss, 10 per cent, is in the control group. Eight cases show a loss in comparison to their controls, and nine reveal a gain. On the whole, there is some significance in the small net improvement manifested by the test group. The average is 2·02 P. E.'s, and the median 4·40 P. E.'s.

The dynamometer results show no gain in strength of grip six months after operation. Indeed the average of the gains of the operative cases is slightly less than the average gain of the controls. Comparing the test group with the control, we find the average of the differences to be -·24. But the variability is so high (P. E. = ±·48) as to render this figure unreliable. The greatest loss in strength of grip is found in the control group, but the greatest gain is also in this group. Seven cases in the test group show a loss, as compared with only three control cases. In eight, or one-half of the sixteen cases, the control member of a pair gained more than the test member. Considering the three pairs of nutrition cases, we find that in pair number 7 the test case loses 1·5 Kg. when compared with the control; and in pair number 10, 6·5 Kg., while the test case in pair 11 gains 4 Kg. The conclusion from the data would seem to be that, within the space of six months at any rate, operation for adenoids and tonsils brings about no increase in strength of grip.

TABLE V

SHOWING CHANGE IN PER CENT OVER OR UNDERWEIGHT FOR HEIGHT AND AGE, 18 PAIRS.

			A			B	A-B
N[‡]	1	2	3	4	5	6	7
8	- 1	- 1	0	-13	- 5	+ 8	- 8
11	- 3	-12	-9	- 9	-11	- 2	- 7
10	- 1	- 5	-4	- 6	- 8	- 2	- 2
28	- 7	- 7	0	0	+ 2	+ 2	- 2
13	-13	-19	-6	-11	-15	- 4	- 2
19	+ 6	+ 8	+2	+ 1	+ 5	+ 4	- 2
6	+ 2	- 3	-5	+ 5	+ 1	- 4	- 1
14	-13	- 9	+4	- 5	0	+ 5	- 1
7	- 8	-15	-7	- 7	-14	- 7	0
2	- 8	- 6	+2	+ 9	+10	+ 1	+ 1
3	+ 6	+ 8	+2	- 5	- 8	- 3	+ 5
16	-16	-15	+1	-13	-17	- 4	+ 5

25	- 8	- 7	+1	+ 4	- 1	- 5	+ 6
5	- 4	- 1	+3	+ 8	+ 4	- 4	+ 7
9	- 8	-11	-3	- 7	-17	-10	+ 7
26	- 1	+ 5	+6	+ 1	0	- 1	+ 7
4	- 7	- 7	0	-15	-23	- 8	+ 8
1	0	+ 8	+8	+ 8	+ 4	- 4	+12
Av.	- 4·67	- 4·94	- ·28	- 3·06	- 5·17	- 2·11	+ 1·83
M			+ ·5			- 3·50	+ 4·00
75%ile			+2			0.00	+ 6·50
25%ile			-2			- 4·50	- 2.00
Q			2			2·25	+ 4·25
P. E. (distribution)			3			2.39	+ 1·33
P. E. (average)			± ·71			± ·57	± ·91

Av.=2·02 P. E.

M.=4·40 P. E.

Is there, after operation, an improvement in motor control and attention, and a lessening of fatiguability as these may be demonstrated in the tapping test? Table VI gives the number of taps in the first half minute of tapping for both groups before and after the six months interval. The test group suffers an average loss of 2·24 taps, and a median loss of 2· The average loss of the control group is 2·33, and the median 2·

TABLE VI

GAIN IN GRIP — 6 MONTHS — 16 PAIRS

N[8]	Test Group (A)			Control Group (B)			
	Test 1	Test 2	Gain	Test 1	Test 2	Gain	
10	12·5	11	-1·5	10	15	5	-6·5
27	9	6	-3	8	9	1	-4
1	13	12	-1	11	13	2	-3
14	16	15	-1	22	24	2	-3
2	9	9	0	10	12	2	-2
9	10·5	13	2·5	16·5	21	4·5	-2
7	7	6·5	- ·5	9	10	1	-1·5
16	19	17·5	-1·5	10	10	0	-1·5
3	12·8	14·5	1·7	14	15	1	·7
13	26·5	28·5	2	22	23	1	1
24	19	20	1	15	15	0	1
19	22	21	-1	15	12	-3	2

22	18	22·5	4·5	19·5	21·5	2	2·5
11	11	15	4	11·5	11·5	0	4
21	16·5	16·5	0	19	15	-4	4
23	11·5	15·5	4	14·5	14	- ·5	4·5
Av.	14·58	15·22	·62	14·19	15·06	·875	- ·24
M			0			1	-1·0
75%ile			3			2	-2·25
25%ile			-1			0	-2·50
Q			2			1	-2·38
P. E. (distribution)			1·58			1·02	-2·49
P. E. (average)			±·40			±·26	± ·48

Av.= -·50 P. E.

M.= -2·08 P. E.

There is practically no change then in the tapping ability of either group. The high unreliability of the difference (P. E. = ± 3·10) is noteworthy. It would seem that incidental causes have a much greater effect upon tapping ability than can be demonstrated as resulting from the removal of adenoids and tonsils.

Use of the tapping test as a measure of the decrease in tendency to fatigue similarly brings out no indication of any improvement in the operative group of cases. The measure of fatigue was taken as a ratio; namely, the number of taps in the first, minus the number in the second half minute over the number of taps in the first half minute. Then, if there is a greater number of taps in the second, the ratio will be minus, indicating that fatigue effect is so small as to be overcome by practice effect. This was a fact in only four cases. Since what we are measuring is improvement, the ratio for test 2 is subtracted from the ratio for test 1 to find the gain in overcoming fatigue. Table VIII shows the average gain for group one to be -·0196, and the median -·045. That is, there is an average increase in fatiguability of ·0196 units and a median increase of ·045 with a P. E. of ± ·02. This increase in fatiguability occurs also in the control group, average 0, and median ·03 with P. E. of ± ·03. The average gain of test group over control group is -·02 and the median gain is -·015. Again variability is relatively large, P. E. being 1·04, so that the median and average gains are -·50 P. E. and -·38 P. E. respectively.

We may say, then, that the capacities brought out by the tapping test seem to undergo no improvement in six months after removal of adenoids and tonsils.

The main line of interest in the present experiment lay with the relation of adenoid and tonsil defects to general intelligence. The results of the two tests dealing more specifically with this side of the problem are here set forth. Table IX shows the I.Q's. of the two groups before and after the six months' interval, together with changes plus or minus in I.Q., and a comparison of the separate pairs in respect to improvement.

We find that the test group shows an average gain in I.Q. of 2·25 points. The median gain is 2 points, the total range 18 points and P. E. of the average is ± ·99.

The control group shows an average gain very slightly higher, 3·25 points, the median gain being 3. The range in this case is 32 points, but P. E. is only ± ·47. The average of the compared gains of separate pairs is -1·035. These numbers are so small as to be insignificant. Actually, we may say that the operative group as a whole showed no gain over the control group. If we examine individual cases we find that the greatest loss in I.Q. was in the control group, (8 points) but the greatest gain (24 points) also appears in this group. In the test group 11 cases

TABLE VII

GAIN IN NUMBER OF TAPS IN ONE-HALF MINUTE, 21 PAIRS — RIGHT HAND

N[¶]	Test Group (A)			Control Group (B)			
	Test 1	Test 2	Gain	Test 1	Test 2	Gain	
14	190	138	-52	175	175	0	-52
10	68	88	20	70	135	65	-45
23	150	141	- 9	122	140	18	-27
1	135	120	-15	106	115	9	-24
9	149	135	-14	144	150	6	-20
21	152	132	-20	140	138	- 2	-18
22	164	183	19	120	157	37	-18
24	157	142	-15	155	155	0	-15
27	108	97	-11	115	112	- 3	- 8
20	105	110	5	150	155	5	0
15	172	170	- 2	140	137	- 3	1
26	137	138	1	125	125	0	1
25	140	150	10	148	151	3	7
3	136	139	3	135	129	- 6	9
13	160	142	-18	150	122	-28	10
18	133	135	2	100	84	-16	18
28	150	162	12	178	170	- 8	20
8	113	110	- 3	131	101	-30	27
11	125	98	-27	155	101	-54	27
2	105	112	7	152	114	-38	45
17	90	150	60	125	121	- 4	64
Av.	135·19	132·95	- 2·24	136·47	134·14	- 2·33	·09
M			-2			-2	0
75%ile			6·5			4·5	16·0
25%ile			-15			-14	19·50
Q			10·75			9·25	17·75

P. E. (distribution)	12·24	7·33	18·09
P. E. (average)	2·66	±1·59	±3·10

Av.= ·03 P. E.
M.= 0 P. E.

lost in I.Q., as compared with 7 in the control group. Thirteen test cases lost in comparison with their respective controls. Two gained equally with their controls, and the remaining thirteen showed a larger gain. In regard to the three pairs taken from the nutrition class, number 7 gained 8 points and his control, 4. Number 10 lost a point and his control lost 4, while number 11 lost 3 points with a gain of 1 point by his control. So that these cases, in spite of most favorable conditions, show no consistent gain in I.Q.

The results of the Healy tests are similar. There is a slightly higher average gain in the control group. The test group contains eight cases which made a poorer score at the end of the interval, the control group six. The range of gains is from -22 to +44, or 66 points, in the test group, while in the control group the gains range from -14 to +41·5 or 55·5

TABLE VIII

DECREASE IN FATIGUE IN TAPPING—DIFFERENCE IN RATES OF SECOND HALF MINUTE OVER FIRST HALF MINUTE. SIXTEEN PAIRS

N[**]	Test Group (A)			Control Group (B)			
	Test 1	Test 2	Gain	Test 1	Test 2	Gain	
13	-·03	·05	-·08	·27	-·28	·55	-·63
28	·01	·11	-·10	·17	·04	·13	-·23
20	·10	·15	-·05	·20	·04	·16	-·21
10	-·09	·07	-·16	·23	·19	·04	-·20
17	·01	·33	-·32	·07	·20	-·13	-·19
25	·09	·21	-·12	·09	·11	-·02	-·10
11	·28	·11	·17	·19	-·06	·25	-·08
15	·03	·08	-·05	·18	·16	·02	-·07
22	·10	·23	-·13	·03	·19	-·16	·03
27	·15	·05	·10	·09	·03	·06	·04
14	·09	·06	·03	·02	·06	-·04	·07
18	·14	·18	-·04	·01	·12	-·11	·07
24	·13	·11	·02	·13	·35	-·22	·24
26	·18	·15	·03	·16	·37	-·21	·24
23	·21	·04	·17	·06	·21	-·15	·32
21	·27	·05	·22	·03	·20	-·17	·39

Av.	·104	·124	-·020	·121	·121	·0	-·020
M			·045			-·03	-0·015
	75%ile		+·03			+·04	·07
	25%ile		-·12			-·16	-·20
Q			·075			·10	·135
P. E. (distribution)			·09			·11	·05
P. E. (average)			±·02			±·03	±·04

Av.= -·50 P. E.

M.= -·38 P. E.

points. Seventeen of the operative cases showed a smaller gain than their respective controls. The three pairs of cases from the nutrition class show the following gains:—pair 7; the test case loses 22 points, the control gains 23 points; pair 10,
test case gains 18·5, but control gains 38 points; pair 11, test case gains 14 points,
and control gains 25·5 points. From this test then, we can find no general tendency
for cases operated on to improve in intelligence in excess of improvement in a
control group which was not so treated.

This question presents itself:—is there any relationship between improvement
in physical well-being as revealed in weight, and improvement in intelligence? If,
as has been supposed, adenoids and diseased tonsils cause mental retardation in-
directly through physical deprivation, it would seem as though greater improvement in intelligence after operation should accompany greater improvement in
weight, and smaller intelligence gain should accompany slighter gain in weight.
In order to determine whether this was true for our cases, improvement in I.Q. was
correlated with gain in weight, for the test group. The order of merit method was
used, and the formula $\varrho = 1 - ((6\Sigma D\_n) /(n(n^2-1)))$ where $f = 2 \sin (\Pi/6)\varrho$. The resulting value of r was -·10 with unreliability of ·226, calculated by the formula $\sigma t.r$
- obt.r = $(1·05(1-r^2)) / \sqrt{n}$. There is therefore no correlation between improvement in
intelligence and gain in weight.

TABLE IX

IMPROVEMENT IN I.Q., 28 PAIRS

N[††]	Test Group (A)			Control Group (B)			
Test 1	Test 2	Gain	Test 1	Test 2	Gain		
27	110	109	-1	72	96	24	-25
20	106	102	-4	118	131	13	-17
8	91	86	-5	98	104	6	-11
24	131	124	-7	89	92	3	-10
21	64	67	3	86	97	11	-8
3	94	91	-3	82	85	3	-6
12	98	95	-3	98	101	3	-6

23	85	94	9	81	96	15	-6
11	103	100	-3	101	102	1	-4
15	97	94	-3	78	79	1	-4
18	98	98	0	90	94	4	-4
4	96	96	0	83	85	2	-2
26	80	76	-4	90	88	-2	-2
16	65	73	8	74	82	8	0
28	81	84	3	95	98	3	0
5	95	99	4	114	117	3	1
2	107	114	7	91	96	5	2
10	110	109	-1	104	100	-4	3
17	71	77	6	96	99	3	3
7	91	99	8	95	99	4	4
1	82	83	1	80	76	-4	5
6	95	101	6	88	89	1	5
19	96	101	5	98	98	0	5
9	83	93	10	87	90	3	7
25	77	76	-1	145	137	-8	7
13	70	78	8	66	64	-2	10
22	91	100	9	63	62	-1	10
14	96	107	11	140	137	3	14
Av.	91·53	93·78	2·25	92·93	96·21	3·285	-1·035
M			2			-1	-0·015
	75%ile		7			+·04	5
	25%ile		-3			-·16	-6
Q			5			2·5	5·5
P. E. (distribution)			5·25			2·5	5
P. E. (average)			±·99			±·47	±1·10

Av.= -·94 P. E.

M.= -·99 P. E.

TABLE X

IMPROVEMENT IN PERFORMANCE OF HEALY TEST, 24 PAIRS

N[‡‡]	Test Group (A)			Control Group (B)			
	Test 1	Test 2	Gain	Test 1	Test 2	Gain	
7	- 6	-28	-22	4·5	27·5	23	-45
13	43	42	- 1	- 1·5	30·5	-32	-33

17	29·5	12	17·5	1·5	15	- 13·5	-31
15	7	25	18	1	42·5	41·5	23·5
26	22·5	7	-15·5	56	61·5	5·5	-21·5
10	-12	6·5	18·5	27	65	38	-19·5
19	57·5	49	- 8·5	-22	-11	11	-19·5
24	54·5	63	8·5	31·5	59·5	28	-19·5
20	0	-11	-11	30	35	5	-16
9	3·5	10·5	7	34	55	21	-14
11	-8	6	14	-29	-3·5	25·5	-11·5
16	49	47·5	- 1·5	30	37	7	- 8·5
1	-25	2	27	-50	-16	34	- 7
22	48·5	43·5	- 5	34·5	33·5	- 1	- 4
18	-13·5	-12	1·5	-32	-28	4	- 2·5
23	49·5	68	18·5	4	25	21	- 2·5
3	21·5	22·5	1	17	19	2	- 1
12	20	21	1	-10	-12	- 2	3
14	12·5	48·5	36	- 5	25·5	30·5	6·5
27	-25	15	40	2	27·5	25·5	14·5
2	28·5	30	1·5	3	-11	-14	15·5
25	8	25	17	29·5	29	-·5	17·5
21	20	32	12	70·5	58·5	-12	24
28	29·5	73·5	44	64·5	51·5	-13	57
Av.	17·29	24·94	7·64	12·12	25·69	13·56	- 5·85
M			4.25			- 7·75	-0·015
75%ile			18			+·04	3
25%ile			-5			-·16	-19·5
Q			11·5			13	11·25
P. E. (distribution)			10·6			10·56	13·65
P. E. (average)			±2·16			± 2·16	± 3·05

Av.= -1·92 P. E.
M.= -2·54 P. E.

Similarly, it might be thought that the children who had suffered from the defects for a comparatively short time, might reveal greater improvement in intelligence after six months than those who had been afflicted for a longer space of time. We had no way of knowing definitely how long the defects had been present in the cases studied. Roughly, though, we may say that in general the older boys have had defective tonsils and adenoids for a longer time than the younger ones, and that the older the boy, the older the defect. On this basis, if correlation of youth with gain in I.Q. should give a larger positive value for r, we might be justified in saying that the younger boys, who have been handicapped for a lesser period, show greater mental recuperation than their older companions. Such a correlation was attempted in the test group, correlating age at the first test with gain in I.Q. The same methods and formulae were used as in the weight and intelligence comparison, the greatest gain in I.Q. being given first position, and the lowest age. The resulting value for r was -·24, with an unreliability of ·186. The relationship would appear to be in the other direction but it is so small, with an unreliability measure so large as to be insignificant. Once more, then, we find in our results no correspondence between recency of defect and quick mental recovery.

TABLE XI

SHOWING PERCENTILE RATINGS OF THE MEMBERS OF THE TWO GROUPS AT THE BEGINNING AND END OF THE SIX MONTHS' INTERVAL

	Weight		Height		Grip		Tapping	
1	·29	·44	·25	·40	·47	·40	·51	·33
1C	·43	·54	·27	·45	·33	·47	·17	·30
2	·04	·10	·04	·11	·16	·16	·16	·25
2C	·38	·55	·20	·32	·25	·40	·80	·28
3	·46	·59	·32	·49	·44	·56	·52	·58
3C	·65	·69	·74	·81	·54	·67	·51	·42
4	·33	·44	·39	·52	·16		·13	
4C	·27	·32	·51	·78	·18		·19	
5	·16	·20	·18	·20	·33		·23	
5C	·50	·53	·28	·47	·40		·87	
6	·12	·15	·06	·10	·10		·23	
6C	·31	·40	·22	·38	·27		·41	
7	·03	·07	·05	·15	·07	·06	·40	·27
7C	·01	·02	·03	·07	·16	·24	·16	
8	·62	·71	·63	·75	·24		·27	·23
8C	·18	·37	·31	·40	·67	·72	·43	·11
9	·31	·41	·47	·53	·26	·47	·71	·51
9C	·60	·65	·76	·89	·76	·89	·63	·78
10	·26	·35	·26	·43	·44	·33	·01	·04
10C	·21	·22	·23	·37	·24	·67	·02	·51
11	·24	·23	·25	·43	·33	·67	·40	·08
11C	·08	·09	·09	·17	·36	·36	·86	·11
12	·25	·40	·15		·53		·08	
12C	·06	·15	·02	·08	·04	·01	·12	·03

N	I.Q.		Healy		Total		Possible	Average Gain
13	·95	1·00	·99	1·00	·99	1·00	·90	·66
13C	·87	·89	·93	·96	·94	·96	·78	·36
14	·49	·66	·67	·74	·72	·67	1·00	·57
14C	·92	·93	·96	·98	·93	·98	·97	·97
15	·56		·68		·70		·95	·94
15C	·79	·80	·59	·66	·67	·70	·62	·54
16	·49	·53	·74	·79	·81	·77	·69	
16C	·34	·28	·50	·54	·24	·24	·69	·51
17	·53		·50		·53		·05	·78
17C	·17		·15		·24	·11	·40	·34
18	·57		·38		·33		·45	·51
18C	·17	·20	·30	·34	·10	·06	·09	·03
19	·95	·99	·94	·98	·94	·88	·93	
19	·38	·45	·30	·37	·67	·40	·09	·31
20	·13		·37		·33		·16	·23
20C	·63	·75	·56	·88	·67	·44	·78	·86
21	·83	·89	·84		·76	·76	·80	·44
21C	·67	·77	·55	·61	·81	·67	·62	·57
22	·85		·81	·91	·78	·95	·92	·99
22C	·83	·92	·93	·97	·82	·91	·33	·89
23	·36		·45		·36	·70	·78	·63
23C	·73	·74	·70	·82	·55	·53	·36	·62
24	·59	·69	·67		·81	·85	·89	·66
24C	·62	·63	·59	·71	·67	·67	·86	·86
25	·47	·60	·57	·63	·53		·62	·78
25C	·73	·74	·60	·64	·44	·91	·70	·79
26	·74	·89	·74	·85	·53		·54	·57
26C	·76	·81	·70	·79	·84	·76	·40	·40
27	·11		·23		·16	·04	·18	·06
27C	·07	·12	·12	·23	·10	·16	·30	·25
28	·86	·90	·87	·90	·97	·88	·78	·91
28C	·87	·93	·83	·86	·88		·98	·94

TABLE XI (CONTINUED)

SHOWING PERCENTILE RATINGS OF THE TWO GROUPS AT THE BEGINNING AND END OF THE SIX MONTHS' INTERVAL

N[§§]

1	·25	·27	·10	·29	·30	415	·05
1C	·21	·15	·01	·12	·53	462	·089
2	·84	·89	·60	·66	·38	416	·063
2C	·45	·51	·29	·18	-·07	358	-·011
3	·49	·44	·49	·51	·40	328	·066
3C	·25	·32	·44	·45	·30	287	·05
4	·59	·59	·38		·22	168	·073
4C	·27	·32	·71		·42	195	·14
5	·53	·71	·10		·42	213	·14
5C	·89	·90	·77		·24	133	·08
6	·53	·77	·02		·55	229	·183
6C	·37	·38	·04		·27	210	·09
7	·45	·71	·22	·07	·37	478	·062
7C	·53	·71	·34	·59	·74	393	·148
8	·45	·34	·70		-·50	303	-·125
8C	·67	·81	·33	·52	·10	241	·025
9	·27	·46	·23	·39	·71	375	·118
9C	·35	·40	·73	·89	·72	217	·12
10	·88	·86	·15	·35	·34	400	·056
10C	·81	·73	·57	·97	1·39	392	·218
11	·79	·73	·20	·34	·21	379	·035
11C	·77	·79	·05	·23	-·44	379	-·073
12	·67	·53	·47	·49	-·11	161	-·036
12C	·67	·77	·19	·15	·19	208	·032
13	·09	·19	·79	·78	·02	129	·003
13C	·06	·05	·24	·67	·06	178	·01
14	·59	·84	·41	·84	·69	212	·115
14C	·97	·96	·21	·56	·41	104	·068
15	·62	·49	·38	·55	·12	106	·04
15C	·19	·20	·26	·79	·66	193	·11
16	·05	·12	·86	·82	·15	205	·03
16C	·13	·25	·66	·76	·24	313	·04
17	·09	·17	·63	·40	·66	223	·220
17C	·59	·71	·27	·43	·21	174	·053
18	·67	·67	·13	·15	·08	175	·027
18C	·40	·49	·04	·07	·18	247	·03
19	·59	·69	·91	·85	·16	67	·032
19C	·67	·67	·11	·18	·16	287	·027

20	·82	·79	·25	·18	-·06	177	-·02
20C	·91	·94	·66	·75	·20	65	·066
21	·05	·07	·47	·69	-·16	209	-·032
21C	·34	·62	·99	·92	·46	157	·077
22	·45	·73	·84	·81	·87	120	·174
22C	·03	·02	·74	·72	·74	275	·123
23	·32	·49	·86	·98	·65	168	·163
23C	·23	·59	·33	·50	1·26	253	·21
24	·94	·92	·88	·95	- ·06	89	-·012
24C	·38	·46	·68	·93	·54	179	·09
25	·17	·15	·37	·55	·49	280	·098
25C	1·00	·97	·63	·60	·53	134	·088
26	·21	·15	·51	·36		226	0
26C	·40	·37	·90	·94	·04	184	·007
27	·88	·86	·10	·43	·05	268	·013
27C	·11	·59	·29	·59	1·49	320	·25
28	·23	·29	·63	1·00	·59	153	·097
28C	·53	·67	·96	·87	·24	83	·048

Table XI expresses the results of Table II, with the scores given in percentile values. In each test, the group was taken as composed of the two scores of every individual—the total number of scores in tests and retests, eliminating those scores where the other member of the pair was lacking, or where no retest was given. Thus case number 1 was just within the lowest 27% of the group in weight at the first weighing, but had advanced to the 44 percentile at the second. In height he gained from the 25 percentile to the 40 percentile. His total gain in all tests is 30 percentile out of a possible 415, and the average gain is ·05. The reader may see by scanning the table that the gains in the test group are practically equaled by those in the control group. There seems to be no consistent relationship between a low score in the first test and a large gain. This is true even though the method of calculation tends to minimize gains at the high end of the group, and losses at the low end. In table XII this may be seen more clearly in respect to I.Q. and the results for all the tests taken together with the I.Q. weighted by being counted twice. A large possible gain indicates that the score at the first testing was low, and vice versa. Considering I.Q. values, the largest possible gain in the test group was 95 per cent of the group. This occurred twice, in one case the actual gain being 7% of the group and in the other 2%. In the control group, the largest possible gain was 97% of the group, but actually this case fell 1% of the group. If we correlate possible gain with actual gain for each group, using the formula $r = 2\sin((\Pi/6)\varrho)$ when $\varrho = 1 - ((6\Sigma D^2)/(n(n^2-1)))$ we get a coefficient of correlation ·36 in the test group, and ·19

TABLE XII

SHOWING GAINS IN PERCENTILE RATING FOR I.Q., AND FOR A TOTAL OF ALL THE TESTS WITH I.Q. WEIGHTED BY BEING COUNTED TWICE.

	I.Q.		A	B	Total		
	1st P.R.	2d P.R.	possible gain	actual gain	possible gain	actual gain	Av. Gain
1	25	27	75	2	415	30	5
1C	21	15	79	-6	462	53	8·9
2	84	89	16	5	416	38	6·3
2C	45	51	55	6	358	- 7	-1·1
3	49	44	51	-5	328	40	6·6
3C	25	32	75	7	287	30	5
4	59	59	41		168	22	7·3
4C	27	32	73	5	195	42	14
5	53	71	47	18	213	42	14
5C	89	90	11	1	133	24	8
6	53	77	47	24	229	55	18·3
6C	37	38	63	1	210	27	9
7	45	71	55	26	478	37	6·2
7C	53	71	47	18	393	74	14·8
8	45	34	55	-11	203	-50	-12·5
8C	67	81	33	14	241	10	2·5
9	27	46	73	19	375	71	11·8
9C	35	40	65	5	217	72	12
10	88	86	12	-2	400	34	5·6
10C	81	73	19	-8	392	139	21·8
11	79	73	21	-6	379	21	3·5
11C	77	79	23	2	379	-44	-7·3
12	67	53	33	- 6	161	- 11	- 3·6
12C	67	77	33	10	208	19	3·2
13	9	19	91	10	129	2	·3
13C	6	5	94	- 1	178	6	1
14	59	84	41	25	212	69	11·5
14C	97	96	3	- 1	104	41	6·8
15	62	49	38	-13	106	12	4
15C	19	20	81	1	193	66	11
16	5	12	95	7	205	15	3

16C	13	25	87	12	213	24	4
17	9	17	81	8	223	66	22
17C	59	71	41	12	174	21	5·3
18	67	67	33		175	8	2·7
18C	40	49	60	9	247	18	3
19	59	69	41	10	67	16	3·2
19C	67	67	33		287	16	2·7
20	82	79	18	- 3	177	-6	- 2
20C	91	94	9	3	65	20	6·6
21	5	7	95	2	209	- 16	- 3·2
21C	34	62	66	28	157	46	7·7
22	45	73	55	28	120	87	17·4
22C	3	2	97	- 1	275	74	12·3
23	32	49	68	17	168	65	16·3
23C	23	59	77	36	253	126	21
24	94	92	6	- 2	89	-6	- 1·2
24C	38	46	62	8	179	54	9
25	17	15	83	- 2	280	49	9·8
25C	100	97		- 3	134	53	8·8
26	21	15	79	- 6	226		
26C	40	37	60	- 3	184	4	·7
27	88	86	12	- 2	268	5	1·3
27C	11	59	89	48	320	148	25
28	23	29	77	6	153	59	9·7
28C	53	67	47	14	83	24	4·8

in the control group. With the small number of cases involved the probable error is too great to allow either of these measures as indicative of relationship. We may say, then, that there is no definite tendency for those of low I.Q. to improve in six months after operation to a greater degree than those of higher I.Q.

Finally, in order to compare the results of the various tests, the measures of the gains of the test group in excess of the control were, for each test, expressed in terms of P. E. The averages and medians of these measures are collected in Table XIII. They show a very slight tendency toward gain in weight, height, and weight-height-age relationship; neither improvement nor loss in grip, tapping fatigueability and I.Q., and a rather curious tendency to loss in the Healy scores. This latter is very probably not a true measure since performance in the Healy Picture Completion test shows a rather high variability, and the cases are so few as to make the influence of single very high or low scores unduly great.

TABLE XIII

SHOWING IMPROVEMENT IN VARIOUS TESTS OF OPERATIVE GROUP OVER AND ABOVE SUCH IMPROVEMENT IN CONTROL GROUP. EXPRESSED IN TERMS OF P. E.

	Weight	Height	Height-Weight	Grip	Tapping	Tapping fatigue	I.Q.	Healy
	P. E.	P. E.	P. E.	P. E.	P. E.	P. E.	P. E.	P. E.
Average	2·85	1·00	2·02	-·50	·03	-·50	-·94	-1·92
Median	2·80	1·25	·55	-·83	·32	-·50	0.00	-2·54

CHAPTER IV

MEASUREMENT OF IMPROVEMENT AFTER A SECOND INTERVAL OF SIX MONTHS

In view of the fact that one of the experimenters[15] found improvement in school work when her study was extended to cover a second time interval after operation, it was deemed advisable to similarly extend the present investigation in order to determine whether our operated cases showed any improvement after twelve months. To this end, the fifty-six children composing the final groups of the first study, were sought after a second interval of about six months. Conditions made it impossible to give all the retests exactly twelve months from the time of the operation. As a matter of fact, the period ranges from ten to seventeen months. An effort was made to keep the interval between tests equal for the two members of a given pair.

The same tests were given as in the first study. About half of the testing was done by one of the former examiners, but she was obliged to turn the work over to another before it had been completed. The second examiner was highly recommended, and had had training and practical experience in the giving of tests. She was instructed in the methods which had been employed previously, so that conditions were as far as possible kept constant.

The results of the tests are collected in Table XIV. In the first column is given the length of the time interval for each case. It may be seen that the final group was composed of forty-two children, forming twenty-one pairs. There were fifteen pairs which received a second rating in weight; thirteen in height; thirteen in grip; fifteen in tapping, eleven in fatigue as shown by tapping, twenty-one in I.Q., and eighteen in the Healy Test. These numbers while they are smaller than we could wish, would seem to be great enough to indicate

TABLE XIV

RESULTS OF THE TESTS AFTER AN INTERVAL OF FROM 10 TO 17 MONTHS

N[¶¶]	Mos.	Weight		Height		Grip	
		Test 1	Test 3	Test 1	Test 3	Test 1	Test 3

---

[15] A. H. MacPhail, Adenoids and Tonsils: A study showing how the Removal of Enlarged or Diseased Tonsils Affects a Child's Work in School. Ped. Sem., June, 1920, pp. 188-194.

1	15	50·4	63·5	46·0	49·7	13·0	18·0
1C	15	53·5	62·8	46·4	49·7	11·0	15·0
2	15	40·9	47·9	42·6	45·9	9·0	10·0
2C	17	52·3	65·5	45·2	49·8	10·0	15·0
3	16	55·0	67·5	47·0	50·2	12·8	13·0
3C	14	61·5	57·8	51·7	54·0	14·0	14·5
4	13	51·1	60·2	47·5	50·5	9·0	
4C	13	49·4	54·2	48·9	50·8	9·5	
7	14	39·9	45·8	42·9	45·6	7·0	6·0
7C	12	38·4	42·1	41·9	43·7	9·0	14·0
8	11	60·8	69·2	50·8	52·3	10·0	
8C	11	45·4	57·9	36·8	48·7	15·0	
10	11	48·9	56·7	46·1	48·6	12·5	12·0
10C	11	47·1	51·8	45·6	48·1	10·0	12·0
11	12	47·8	55·0	45·8	49·5	11·0	11·0
11C	12	41·6	47·0	43·6	46·8	11·5	7·5
12	12	48·0	66·5	44·8		14·0	
12C	11	41·0	69·6	41·5		6·0	
13	12	90·0	112·0	61·3	61·8	26·5	28·5
13C	12	74·7	88·0	56·8	60·0	22·0	27·0
14	12	56·0	66·0	51·0	53·3	16·0	17·0
14C	12	81·9	98·0	57·9	59·5	22·0	22·5
15	12	57·5		51·1		15·5	
15C	10	67·2		50·1		15·0	
16	12	56·0	60·3	51·6	53·5	19·0	18·5
16C	11	51·2	55·0	48·7	50·1	10·0	10·0
18	12	58·2		47·3		18·0	
18C	11	45·3		46·7		8·0	
19	12	90·0	108·0	57·7	60·5	22·0	20·0
19C	11	52·4	59·0	46·7	48·0	15·0	18·0
20	12	44·2		47·2		11·0	
20C	11	61·3		49·6		15·0	
21	12	70·7	85·5	54·1		16·5	15.0
21C	10	62·4	69·2	49·6		19·0	17·0
23	12	51·7		47·8		11·5	15·0
23C	11	64·1		51·4		14·5	16·0
27	12	43·7		45·4		9·0	6·0
27C	11	41·0		44·6		0	9·0

28	12	71·3	78·5	54·9	56·3	23·5
28C	11	74·2	85·8	53·4	55·9	21·0

N[***]	Tapping		I.Q.		Healy	
	Test 1	Test 3	(1)	(3)	(1)	(3)
1	135	142	82	93·0	-25·0	11·0
1C	106	134	80	85·0	-50·0	11·0
2	105	135	107	113·0	28·5	24·5
2C	152	139	91	86·0	3·0	19·5
3	136	144	94	91·0	21·5	15·5
3C	135	135	82	96·0	17·0	25·5
4	103		96	111	8·5	
4C	109		83	102	33·0	
7	125		91	93	- 6·0	16·0
7C	105		95	112	4·5	11·0
8	113	128	91	92·0	32·5	
8C	131	121	98	111·0	4·0	
10	68+ 74	145+106	110	116·0	-12·0	11·0
10C	70+ 74	148+124	104	107·0	27·0	48·5
11	125+ 90	120+125	103	102·0	- 8·0	15·5
11C	155+125	102+112	101	95·0	-29·0	-20·0
12	98+ 69			86	20·0	1·0
12C	102		98	90	-10·0	41·5
13	160+165	176+187	70	61·0	43·0	62·5
13C	150+109	188+174	66	60·0	-1·5	21·5
14	190+172	228+215	96	102·0	12·5	77·0
14C	175+152	165+186	140	138·0	- 5·0	48·5
15	172+167	192+186	97	97·0	7·0	19·0
15C	140+115	145+133	78	98·0	1·0	54·5
16	145+131		65	74	49·0	79·0
16C	145+ 99		74	81	30·0	45·5
18	133+115	126+145	98	101·0	-13·5	13·5
18C	100+ 99	108+ 92	90	92·0	-32·0	-35·0
19	168+136		96	97	57·5	60·5
19C	100+115		98	90	-22·0	-15·0
20	105+115	122+118	106	116·0		55·0
20C	150+120	154+154	118	140·0	30·0	48·5
21	152+111	154+155	64	66·0	20·0	38·0

21C	140+136	174+150	86	93·0	70·5	88·0
23	150+119	157+157	85	80·0	49·5	62·5
23C	122+115	141+141	81	88·0	4·0	64·0
27	108+ 92	114+ 95	110	112·0	-25·0	25·5
27C	115+105	101+118	72	98·0	2·0	39·5
28	150+148	176+168	81	83·0	29·5	77·5
28C	178+148	172+157	95	94·0	64·5	83·5

any very consistent tendency toward improvement. The question, whether or not the results are affected by the differences in time interval, will be considered later.

In weight, the test group showed an average gain of 11·013 pounds, with a median of 9·1 (Table XV). The average gain of the control group was 9·113 pounds and the median 6·8. The gains in the test group are less variable than those of the control. The average of the gains of the test group in excess of those of the control is 1·9 pounds, and the median is 2·2 pounds; while the unreliability of the difference is ± 1·46 The average, then, is only 1·30 P. E. and the median 1·51 P. E.

If we turn to Table III and compare the results there set forth with the results at the end of the second period, we find the gains of the test group exceed those of the control in the following manner.

TABLE XV

WEIGHT, SECOND RETESTS, 15 PAIRS

N[††††]	Test Group (A)			Control Group (B)			
	Test 1	Test 3	Gain	Test 1	Test 3	Gain	A-B
12	48	66·5	18·5	69·6	28·6	-10·1	
2	40·9	47·9	7	52·3	65·5	13·2	-6·2
14	56	66	10	81·9	98	16·1	-6·1
28	71·3	78·5	7·2	74·2	85·8	11·6	-4·4
8	60·8	69·2	8·4	45·4	57·9	12·5	-4·1
16	56	60·3	3·7	51·2	55	3·8	-·1
11	47·8	55	7·2	41·6	47	5·4	1·8
7	39·9	45·8	5·9	38·4	42·1	3·7	2·2
10	48·9	56·7	7·8	47·1	51·8	4·7	3·1
1	50·4	63·5	13·1	53·5	62·8	9·3	3·8
4	51·1	60·2	9·1	49·4	54·2	4·8	4·3
21C	70·7	85·5	14·8	62·4	69·2	6·8	8
13	90	112	22	74·7	88	13·3	8·7
19	90	108	18	52·4	59	6·6	11·4
3	55	67·5	12·5	61·5	57·8	-3·7	16·2

Av.	58·45	69·50	11·01	55·13	63·58	9·11	1·9
M			9·1			6·8	2·2
75%ile			13·52			12·67	5·22
25%ile			7·15			4·47	-4·07
Q			3·18			4·1	4·65
P. E. (distribution)			3·81			4·19	6·1
P. E. (average)			±1·00			±1·07	±1·46

Av. = 1·30 P. E.

M. = 1·51 P. E.

	6 months	12 months
Average of gains in test group in excess of control	1·37	1·90
Median	1·20	2·20
P. E. of difference	±·48	±1·46
Average in terms of P. E.	2·85	1·30
Median in terms of P. E.	2·80	1·51

After a twelve months' interval, therefore, the actual average and median gains are slightly larger than after the first six months, but the variability is very much greater. Therefore, when expressed in terms of P. E., the gains are smaller. One of the test group cases (No. 13) who had gained 8 pounds after six months, gained 14 pounds in the second period of six months, making a total gain of 22 pounds. This gain is exceeded, however, by one in the control group (No. 12) who gained 3·5 pounds in six months, and 25·1 pounds more in the ensuing five months. This is certainly an enormous gain for five months, under any circumstances. Turning to Table XIV we find no corresponding gain in I.Q. for this child. Indeed there is a loss of five points.

Other children in the test group who made large gains, were case 12, with a gain of 18·5 pounds after twelve months, compared with 4·5 pounds after six months; case 19, gain of 6·3 pounds after first six months, and 18 pounds after 12 months; case 21, whose gain after the first period was 5·8 pounds, but who gained 14·8 pounds after twelve months. In these cases the gain in the second period greatly exceeds that for the first.

TABLE XVI

HEIGHT, SECOND RETESTS, 13 PAIRS

N[‡‡‡]	Test Group (A)			Control Group (B)			A-B
	Test 1	Test 3	Gain	Test 1	Test 3	Gain	
13	61·3	61·8	·5	56·8	60·0	3·2	-2·7
2	42·6	45·9	3·3	45·2	49·8	4·6	-1·3
28	54·9	56·3	1·4	53·4	55·9	2·5	-1·1

8	50·8	52·3	1·5	46·8	48·7	1·9	- ·4
10	46·1	48·6	2·5	45·6	48·1	2·5	·0
1	46·0	49·7	3·7	46·4	49·7	3·3	·4
11	45·8	49·5	3·7	43·6	46·8	3·2	·5
16	51·6	53·5	1·9	48·7	50·1	1·4	·5
14	51·0	53·3	2·3	57·9	59·5	1·6	·7
3	47·0	50·2	3·2	51·7	54·0	2·3	·9
7	42·9	45·6	2·7	41·9	43·7	1·8	·9
4	47·5	50·5	3·0	48·9	50·8	1·9	1·1
19	57·7	60·5	2·8	46·7	4·8	1·3	1·5
Av.	49·63	52·17	2·5	48·74	51·16	2·42	·08
M			2·7			2·3	·5
75%ile			3·15			2·85	·85
25%ile			1·6			1·75	·92
Q			·775			·65	·885
P. E. (distribution)			·66			·78	·82
P. E. (average)			±·18			±·22	±·28

Av.=·29 P. E.

M.=1·79 P. E.

In weight, then, the mean gain of the test group over and above the control continues to increase through the second period of six months. The variability, however, increases enormously, which fact is due possibly to varying conditions which may enter in during the longer period to affect the health and thus lessen the gain of some of the children.

In order to determine whether the slight inequalities in interval length have any considerable effect on the results, we have calculated the relation between the length of interval and amount of improvement. The coefficient of correlation by the method of rank differences is equal to ·03. The small number of cases renders the unreliability of correlation very great, but we can at least say that there is no consistent relationship between improvement and time interval, within the narrow limits here set. We are probably justified in taking twelve months as the interval, since such was the case in eight out of the fifteen test cases, while the greatest variation above this made was four months, and below it, one month.

The gains in height after twelve months are shown in Table XVI. The average gain of test group in excess of control, is only ·08 inches, and the median ·5 inches. Variability is about the same as at the end of six months, P. E. ± ·28. The average is only ·29 P. E., but the median is a little larger, 1·79 P. E. If these measures are compared with the results after the first period, we have:

           6 months   12 months

Average of gains of test group in excess of control	·16	·08
Median of gains of test group in excess of control	·20	·50
P. E. of difference	·16	·28
Average in terms of P. E.	1·00	·29
Median in terms of P. E.	1·25	1·79

There seems to be little gain in height after the first period. Test cases 1 and 11 each show a gain of 3·7 inches after fifteen and twelve months respectively, compared with gains after six months of 1·6, and 1·9 inches. But case 2 in the control group, makes still greater comparative gain, +1·8 inches after six months and 4·6 inches after seventeen months. In this case there are almost six additional months for the child to grow, which may account for the larger gain. Control case 1, however, may be compared with his partner, mentioned above, since the interval between tests was the same for both. This boy grew 1·4 inches in six months, and 3·3 inches after 15 months. This is practically equal growth with test case 1. Control case 11 also shows relatively great growth during 12 months, +3·2 inches, whereas the growth in six months was only 1·3 inches. Out of the test group, 7 cases gained more in the first period of six months, than in the second, while only 6 gained more in the second than in the first. Of the control group, 7 cases made more than half of their total gain during the second six months of the total twelve months' period. Since this is true, it seems likely that whatever increase in growth we find during the second half of the twelve months' interval, may be explained by incidental causes, and that so far as actual gain in height is considered, there is no further effect from the operations, after six months.

As was mentioned in the previous chapter, height and weight are of less significance when considered alone, than when taken in relation to each other and to the age of the individual. The gain in this weight-height-age relationship following upon operation for adenoids and tonsils, will be considered in the same manner as were weight and height gains. We have, then:

TABLE XVII

HEIGHT-WEIGHT RELATIONSHIP, SECOND RETESTS, 13 PAIRS SHOWING CHANGES IN PER CENT OVER OR UNDERWEIGHT AFTER 12 MONTHS' INTERVAL

N[§§§]	Test Group (A)			Control Group (B)			
	Test 1	Test 3	Change	Test 1	Test 2	Change	A-B
8	- 1	+ 7	+ 8	-13	0	+13	- 5
16	-16	-17	- 1	-13	- 9	+ 4	- 5
11	- 3	- 6	- 3	- 9	-10	- 1	- 2
14	-13	- 6	+ 7	- 5	+ 4	+ 9	- 2
19	+ 6	+10	+ 4	+ 1	+ 7	+ 6	- 2

28	- 7	- 4	+ 3	0	+ 5	+ 5	- 2
10	- 1	0	+ 1	- 6	- 6	0	+ 1
7	- 8	- 8	0	- 7	- 9	- 2	+ 2
2	- 8	- 4	+ 4	+ 9	+10	+ 1	+ 3
4	- 7	- 4	+ 3	-15	-15	0	+ 3
1	0	+ 6	+ 6	+ 8	+ 5	- 3	+ 9
13	-13	+ 6	+19	-11	-12	- 1	+20
3	+ 6	+13	+ 7	- 5	-20	-15	+22
Av.	- 5	-·54	4·46	- 5·08	3·85	1·23	3·23
M			4			- 2	6
75%ile			6·75			2·75	3
25%ile			- 2·50			2·75	- 2
Q			4·625			2·75	2·50
P. E. (distribution)			2·54			3·23	5·23
P. E. (average)			± ·71			± ·90	± 1·15

Av.=2·81 P. E.

M. =5·22 P. E.

	6 months	12 months
Average of gains of test group in excess of control	1·83	3·23
Median of gains of test group in excess of control	4·00	6·00
P. E. of difference	·91	1·15
Average in terms of P. E.	2·02	2·81
Median in terms of P. E.	4·40	5·22

The mean of the actual gains in the second period exceeds that of the first. Again the second group of results is more variable, decreasing the reliability. There seems, however, to be a definite increase in the net gain of the test group during a second six months' period. Some individual cases may be cited. The greatest gain after six months is 8 units in the test case, matched by an equal gain of 8 units in the control group. After twelve months, the test group shows one gain of 19 units, the highest gain in the control group being 13. Six cases in the test group, and 13 in the control had lost at the end of six months, but after twelve months, all but 2 of the test cases showed a gain, and all but 5 of the controls. In 10 test cases out of the total 13, more than half of the gain occurred during the second six months. In the control group, six of the cases made more than half of their gain during the second six months, and the second interval gains of the other 7 cases exceeded the 50 per cent mark by so little that they may be accounted for by chance.

These results seem to indicate a slight but actual increase in the net gain of the test group during the second six months of the experiment, and an accompanying growth in the variability of these gains.

It will be remembered that the results described in the previous chapter show no gain in strength of grip as a result of operation. Comparison of the 13 cases tested after the second interval, with the 16 cases at the end of the first, gives results as follows:

TABLE XVIII
GAIN IN GRIP, SECOND RETEST, 13 PAIRS

N[¶¶¶]	Test Group (A)			Control Group (B)			A-B
	Test 1	Test 2	Gain	Test 1	Test 2	Gain	
7	7	6	-1	9	14	5	-6
19	22	20	-2	15	18	3	-5
2	9	10	1	10	15	5	-4
27	9	6	-3	8	9	1	-4
13	26·5	28·5	2	22	27	5	-3
10	12·5	12	-·5	10	12	2	-2·5
16	19	18·5	-·5	10	10		- ·5
3	12·5	13	·5	14	14·5	·5	
14	16	17	1	22	22·5	·5	·5
21	16·5	15	-1·5	19	17	-2	·5
1	13	18	5	11	15	4	1
23	11·5	15	3·5	14·5	16	1·5	2
11	11	11		11·5	7·5	-4	4
Av.	14·27	14·61	·34	13·54	15·19	1·65	-1·31
M			0			1·5	-1·5
75%ile			1·25			3·75	·62
25%ile			-1·38			·12	-·4
Q			1·31			1·81	·51
P. E. (distribution)			1·34			1·65	2·31
P. E. (average)			± ·37			±·46	±·59

Av.=-2·22 P. E.

M.=-2·54 P. E.

	6 months	12 months
Average of gains of test group in excess of control	-·24	-1·31
Median of gains of test group in excess of control	-1·00	-1·50
P. E. of difference	±·48	±·59

Average in terms of P. E.	-·50	-2·22
Median in terms of P. E.	-2·08	-2·54

The greatest gain in the test group after twelve months is 5 Kg. (Case 1). During the first six months this case lost 1 Kg. There are two gains of 5 Kg. in the control group. Of these two (cases 7 and 13) had gained 1 Kg. during the first interval and another (case 2) 2 Kg. The greatest loss in the test group after the twelve months' period was 3 Kg., by case 27, which had already lost this amount at the end of six months. The greatest loss in the control group was suffered by case 11, a loss of 4 Kg., all in the second period. After the first period, 9 out of 16 cases in the test group gained in strength of grip, and 13 in the control group. After the second period, the test cases showing gain numbered only 7 out of 13, while all of the control cases had gained except 2. Of the test group 8 cases in the second period either gained less than half of the amount they had improved in the first period, or dropped from the scores they had made at that time. The corresponding numbers for the control group are 6 and 7.

There is evidently no improvement in strength of grip twelve months after operation. The unreliability of the results is very great. However, there is certainly no tendency toward improvement. Why this should be is a question. It may be that the change in examiners is partly responsible, for performance in this test is influenced to a surprising extent by the manner in which it is presented.

TABLE XIX

TAPPING — SECOND RETEST, 15 PAIRS

N[****]	Test Group (A)			Control Group (B)			A-B
	Test 1	Test 3	Gain	Test 1	Test 3	Gain	
21	152	154	2	149	174	34	-32
13	160	176	16	150	188	38	-22
1	135	142	7	106	134	28	-21
18	133	126	- 7	100	108	8	-15
23	150	157	7	122	141	19	-12
10	68	145	77	70	148	78	- 1
3	136	144	8	135	135	0	8
20	105	122	17	150	154	4	13
15	172	192	20	140	145	5	15
27	108	114	6	115	101	-14	20
8	113	128	15	131	121	-10	25
28	150	176	26	178	172	- 6	32
2	105	135	30	152	139	-13	43
11	125	120	- 5	155	102	-53	48
14	190	228	38	175	165	-10	48

Av.	133·47	150·6	17·13	134·6	141·8	7·2	9·93
M			15			4	11
75%ile			21·5			21·5	26·75
25%ile			5			-10·75	-16·5
Q			8·25			16·12	21·62
P. E. (distribution)			10·13			17·2	22·07
P. E. (average)			± 2·67			± 4·53	± 5·26
						Av.=1·89 P. E.	
						M. =2·09 P. E.	

There were 15 pairs of cases who performed the tapping test at the end of twelve months. Comparison with the 21 pairs after six months yields the following results:

	6 months	12 months
Average of gains of test group in excess of control	- ·09	9·93
Median of gains of test group in excess of control	0·00	11·00
P. E. of difference	±3·10	± 5·26
Average in terms of P. E.	·03	1·89
Median in terms of P. E.	0·00	2·09

The gain in the second interval is greater for the tapping test than for any of the tests yet described. After the first six months there is no gain. At the end of ten months the average gain is 9·93, and the median 11 taps per half minute. After six months' interval, 11 of 21 test group cases had lost. At the end of twelve months, only 2 out of 15 had lost. The control group, on the other hand, lost in 11 out of 21 cases after six months, and in 6 out of 15 at the end of twelve months. All but one of the test group cases made more than half of their gain in the second period. Of the control group only 7 cases did this. The variability of gains after 12 months is about equal to the variability at the end of six months.

Strangely enough, decrease in fatigueability as described in the previous chapter does not show itself after 12 months. In fact, the negligible loss in ability noticeable after six months has increased after a period of twelve months. In only 4 out of 11 test group cases, is the gain in the second period equal to that of the first, a similar result to that found in the control group, where 5 out of the 11 cases made half their total gain in the second interval. The results are compared below.

	6 months	12 months
Average of gains of test group in excess of control	-·020	- ·060
Median of gains of test group in excess of control	-·015	- ·090

			±·040	± ·036
P. E. of difference			±·040	± ·036
Average in terms of P. E.			-·500	-1·660
Median in terms of P. E.			-·380	-2·500

TABLE XX

TAPPING FOR FATIGUE, SECOND RETESTS, 11 PAIRS

N[†††††]	Test Group (A)			Control Group (B)			
	Test 1	Test 3	Gain	Test 1	Test 3	Gain	A-B
20	-·10	·03	-·13	·20	·0	·20	-·33
27	·15	·17	-·02	·09	-·17	·26	-·28
10	-·09	·27	-·36	·06	·16	-·10	-·26
14	·09	·05	·04	·13	-·13	·26	-·22
13	-·03	-·06	·03	·27	·07	·20	-·17
28	·01	·05	-·04	·17	·10	·07	-·11
15	·03	·03	·0	·18	·08	·10	-·10
23	·11	·0	·11	·06	·0	·06	·05
21	·27	-·01	·28	·29	·14	·15	·13
11	·28	-·04	·32	·11	-·01	·12	·20
18	·14	-·15	·29	·01	·15	-·14	·43
Av.	·078	·031	·047	·143	·035	·107	-·06
M			·03			·12	-·09
75%ile			·153			·20	·07
25%ile			-·062			·02	-·275
Q			·107			·09	·172
P. E. (distribution)			·087			·093	·19
P. E. (average)			±·02			±·03	±·036

Av.=-1·66 P. E.

M.=-2·50 P. E.

The point of greatest interest in the present study is, as has been said, improvement in intelligence. Does operation for adenoids and tonsils result in improvement in intelligence, as measured by I.Q.? If such improvement does not manifest itself after six months, can it be found after a second period of the same length? The latter question is answered by observation of Table XXI and attention to the following facts, gathered from the 21 pairs of cases who were given intelligence tests after the twelve months' interval.

	6 months	12 months
Average of gains of test group in excess of control	-1·035	-3·14

Median of gains of test group in excess of control	-1	-3
P. E. of difference	±1·10	±1·84
Average in terms of P. E.	- ·94	-1·71
Median in terms of P. E.	- ·99	-1·63

The result after twelve months remains the same as that after the six months' interval. A gain or loss of two or three points in I.Q. is negligible, so that the mean gain of the test group in excess of the control is practically zero at the end of each period. Variability increases with the length of the interval. One case in the test group (case 4) gained nothing in six months, but showed a gain of 15 points after 13 months. However, there is a control case to match this, — case 15, who gained 1 point in the first six months and 20 points after 10 months. Case 20 in the test group lost 4 points in the first six months, but gained back these and 10 additional in the second period. But control No. 1 gained 5 points in the second interval after having lost 4 in the first.

On the other hand several cases lost in the second period, as compared with the first. Test group case 7, for example, gained 8 points in the first six months, and lost 6 of them in the second. Case 3 in the same group lost 3 points in the first period, and failed to regain any of them. Case 12 lost 3 points in six months and 9 more before the end of 12 months. In the control group, case 23 gained 15 pounds in the first six months and lost eight of them in the second. Summing up gains and losses in the second period, for both groups:

TABLE XXI

I.Q., SECOND RETESTS, 21 PAIRS

N[‡‡‡‡]	Test Group (A)			Control Group (B)			A-B
	Test 1	Test 3	Gain	Test 1	Test 3	Gain	
27	110	112	2	72	98	26	-24
15	97	97		78	98	20	-20
3	94	91	-3	82	96	14	-17
7	91	93	2	95	112	17	-15
20	106	116	10	118	140	22	-12
23	85	80	-5	81	88	7	-12
8	91	92	1	98	111	13	-12
12	98	86	-12	98	91	-7	-5
21	64	66	2	86	93	7	-5
4	96	111	15	83	102	19	-4
13	70	61	-9	66	60	-6	-3
18	98	101	3	90	92	2	1
16	65	74	9	74	81	7	2

10	110	116	6	104	107	3	3
28	81	83	2	95	94	-1	3
11	103	102	-1	101	95	-6	5
1	82	93	11	80	85	5	6
14	96	102	6	140	138	-2	8
19	96	97	1	98	90	-8	9
2	107	113	6	91	86	-5	11
9	83	102	19	87	91	4	15
Av.	91·5	94·6	3·0	91·2	97·5	6·2	-3·1
M			2			5	-3
75%ile			6			13·75	4·5
25%ile			-·75			-4·25	-12
Q			3·37			9·00	8·25
P. E. (distribution)			2·09			8·24	8·86
P. E. (average)			±·45			±1·79	±1·84
						Av.=-1·71 P. E.	
						M.=-1·63 P. E.	

	Lost in 2nd period	Gained in 2nd period	No change	Gained equally with gain in 1st period
Test group	9	11	1	9
Control group	10	11		8

The average gain of the test group was 3·09 points after 12 months, compared with 2·25 after six. The control group, however, made an average gain of 6·24 after 12 months, the gain after six months being 3·29. These numbers are insignificant as gains, but they at least show no improvement in the test group which the control group does not reveal as well. On the basis of the results, we may say that there has been no improvement in I.Q. as a result of operation, either after six months or after twelve.

There remains to be considered only the result of the Healy Picture Completion Test. We have scores in this test for 18 pairs of cases. When these scores are compared with those in the former tests, the results stand as follows:

Average of gains of test group in excess of control	-5·85	-3·36
Median of gains of test group in excess of control	-7·75	1·00
P. E. of difference	±3·05	±3·38
Average in terms of P. E.	-1·92	-·87
Median in terms of P. E.	-2·54	·26

The figures given above show no gain in the Healy test as a result of operation. Both after six months, and after twelve, we find that the test group has gained no more than the control group. As before there are individual cases showing considerable gain in the second period, but these are matched by control cases which reveal equal or even greater gains. In the test group, 5 cases lost in the second period in comparison with the first, 18 gained, and 7 gained as much in the second period as in the first. The control group lost in the second period in 5 cases, gained in 18, and gained as much as in the first period in 7 cases. The two groups, then, are practically equal, both showing a gain in the second period, but this gain cannot be due to the operations, since the control group did not undergo operation.

TABLE XXII
HEALY A, SECOND RETESTS, 18 PAIRS

N[§§§§]	Test Group (A)			Control Group (B)			A-B
	Test 1	Test 3	Gain	Test 1	Test 3	Gain	
12	20	1	-19	-10	41.5	51.5	-70.5
23	49.5	62.5	13	4	64	60	-47
15	7	19	12	1	54.5	53.5	-41.5
1	-22	11	36	-50	11	61	-25
2	28.5	24.5	-4	3	19.5	16.5	-20.5
3	21.5	15.5	-6	17	25.5	8.5	-14.5
19	57.5	60.5	3	-22	-15	7	-4
13	43	62.5	19.5	-1.5	21.5	23	-3.5
21	20	38	18	70.5	88	17.5	.5
10	-12	11	23	27	48.5	21.5	1.5
14	12.5	77	64.5	-5	48.5	53.5	11
27	-25	25.5	50.5	2	39.5	37.5	13
11	-8	15.5	23.5	-29	-20	9	14.5
16	49	79	30	30	45.5	15.5	14.5
7	-6	16	22	45	11	6.5	15.5
28	29.5	77.5	48	64.5	83.5	19	29
18	-13.5	13.5	27	-32	-35	-3	30
20	0	55	55	30	48.5	18.5	36.5
Av.	13.81	36.92	23.11	5.77	32.25	26.47	-3.36
M			22.5			18.75	1
75%ile			33			44	14.5
25%ile			7.5			8.75	-22.25
Q			12.75			17.62	18.37
P. E. (distribution)			11.5			17.72	17.86
P. E. (average)			±2.7			±4.22	±3.88

Av.=-·87 P. E.

M.=+·26 P. E.

TABLE XXIII

Gains	Weight in pounds		Height in inches			Height-weight percents		Grip in Kg.	
	lb.	P. E.	in.	P. E	%	P. E.	Kg.	P. E.	
Av. 1	1·37	2·85	·16	1·00	1·83	2·02	- ·24	- ·50	
Av. 2	1·90	1·30	·08	·29	3·23	2·81	-1·31	-2·22	
M. 1	1·20	2·80	·20	1·25	4·00	4·40	-1·00	-2·08	
M. 2	2·20	1·51	·50	1·79	6·00	5·22	-1·50	-2·54	
P. E. 1	± ·48		±·16		±·91		±·48		
P. E. 2	±1·46		±·28		±1·15		±·59		

TABLE XXIII (CONTINUED)

Gains	Taps in 1/2 min.		Tapping in fatigue ratios		I.Q.		Healy Score	
	taps	P. E.	ratio	P. E.	Pts.	P. E.	Pts	P. E.
Av. 1	·09	·03	-·02	- ·50	-1·035	- ·94	-5·85	- ·92
Av. 2	9·93	1·89	-·065	-1·66	-3·140	-1·71	-3·36	- ·87
M. 1	0·00	0·00	-·015	- ·38	-1·000	- ·99	-7·75	-2·54
M. 2	11·00	2·09	-·09	-2·50	-3·000	-1·63	1·00	·26
P. E. 1	±3·10		±·040		±1·10		±3·05	
P. E. 2	±5·26		±·036		±1·84		±3·88	

In Table XXIII are collected the results discussed in the foregoing chapter. The mean results are expressed in terms of P. E. and as gross values, so that the various tests may be compared.

CHAPTER V.
SUMMARY.

The results obtained from the experiment may be summarized as follows:

1. Six months after operation for adenoids and tonsils, there seems to be a slight but not very reliable gain in weight as the result of the operation. After twelve months this has increased; indeed, it has very nearly doubled.

2. Gain in height, resulting from operation, is so slight as to be unreliable. This gain does not increase during a second period of six months.

3. The height-weight-age relationship is an excellent measure of the physical well-being of the child. The figures expressing this relationship show no very reliable gain in the first six months, but improvement increases considerably during the second period.

4. The test group shows no gain over the control group in strength of grip. There seems on the other hand to be a slight loss; which does not decrease in amount during the second period.

5. Speed of tapping did not increase during the first period, any more for the test group than for the control. During the second period, however, there is a marked improvement.

6. Operation for adenoids and tonsils does not lessen fatigueability as shown by the tapping test. The probability is, however, that the test is at fault.

7. No rise in I.Q., as a result of operation, makes itself evident after six months or after twelve months.

8. There is no improvement in the performance of the Healy test either after six months or after twelve.

9. In every test except grip and tapping, there is a marked increase in the variability of the gains after the second period. This is possibly due simply to the fact that the longer interval permits the intervention of more extraneous factors which may influence the scores in one direction or the other.

10. A group of 236 children with diseased tonsils showed equal distribution of I.Q. with a group of 294 children who were normal in this respect.

CONCLUSIONS

The article by MacPhail, which has been reviewed in a former chapter, showed pretty conclusively that the removal of adenoids and tonsils was followed by improvement in school work. That such improvement was not due to a rise in general intelligence can be concluded from the present experiment. That efficiency in school work does not rest wholly upon intelligence has been demonstrated more than once. The tendency here noted to improve in general physical tone may, perhaps, serve as a sign of the factor upon which such improvement depends. Improved health means better attention, better emotional response, greater resistance to fatigue, and probably increased efficiency.

Interesting investigations of such improvement in efficiency might be made by administering educational tests to groups similar to those of the present study. The results of such an experiment would be exceedingly instructive, and would be more significant than conclusions drawn from school marks. By this means also we might determine along what special line efficiency is most affected.

Since there was no recuperation in intelligence resulting from operation for adenoids and tonsils, it is reasonable to expect that there had been no retardation from which to recuperate. This supposition is borne out by results of the statistical study, wherein we found that a group of children suffering from diseased tonsils possessed equal intelligence with a group which was free from such defect.

We can say to physicians, then, with fair amount of assurance, that removal of adenoids and tonsils will probably not raise to any great degree the intelligence level of the mentally defective child who is brought to him. We can say to students of the constancy of the I.Q., that it is not greatly lowered by adenoids and diseased tonsils and we may say to the clinical psychologist that these defects have no demonstrable effect upon general intelligence, whatever effects they may have on volitional and emotional normality,—the two elements which, along with intelligence are necessary for the maintenance of the individual as an instrument of social efficiency.

ENDNOTES

[*]   Numbers refer to cases as listed on Table II.

[†]   Numbers refer to cases as listed on Table II.

[‡]   Numbers refer to cases as listed on Table II.

[§]   Numbers refer to cases as listed on Table II.

[¶]   Numbers refer to cases as listed on Table II.

[**]   Numbers refer to cases as listed on Table II.

[††]   Numbers refer to cases as listed on Table II.

[‡‡]   Numbers refer to cases as listed on Table II.

[§§]   Numbers refer to cases as listed on Table II.

[¶¶]   Numbers refer to cases as listed on Table II.

[***]   Numbers refer to cases as listed on Table II.

[†††]   Numbers refer to cases as listed on Table II.

[‡‡‡]   Numbers refer to cases as listed on Table II.

[§§§]   Numbers refer to cases as listed on Table II.

[¶¶¶]   Numbers refer to cases as listed on Table II.

[****]   Numbers refer to cases as listed on Table II.

[††††]   Numbers refer to cases as listed on Table II.

[‡‡‡‡]   Numbers refer to cases as listed on Table II.

[§§§§]   Numbers refer to cases as listed on Table II.

Lector House believes that a society develops through a two-fold approach of continuous learning and adaptation, which is derived from the study of classic literary works spread across the historic timeline of literature records. Therefore, we aim at reviving, repairing and redeveloping all those inaccessible or damaged but historically as well as culturally important literature across subjects so that the future generations may have an opportunity to study and learn from past works to embark upon a journey of creating a better future.

This book is a result of an effort made by Lector House towards making a contribution to the preservation and repair of original ancient works which might hold historical significance to the approach of continuous learning across subjects.

HAPPY READING & LEARNING!

LECTOR HOUSE LLP
E-MAIL: lectorpublishing@gmail.com